Paula Deen's

2009 Calendar

Paula Deen's
2009 Calendar

RANDOM HOUSE
NEW YORK

Published in the United States by Random House,
an imprint of The Random House Publishing Group,
a division of Random House, Inc., New York.

RANDOM HOUSE and colophon
are trademarks of Random House, Inc.

ISBN 978-1-4000-6781-7

Printed in China on acid-free paper

www.atrandom.com

246897531

FIRST EDITION

Calendar design by Breanne Jackson,
Cooking with Paula Deen magazine

Photography courtesy Hoffman Media

Paula Deen's

2009 Calendar

Winter

I can't think of a better time than
the new year to set your sights on
celebrating your life and you! Fresh
starts and fabulous food—what
more can you ask for?

January 2009

Sunday	Monday	Tuesday	Wednesday	Thursday
				New Year's Day 1
4	5	6	7	8
11	12	13	14	15
18	Martin Luther King Jr. Day 19	20	21	22
25	26	27	28	29

Friday	Saturday
2	3
9	10
16	17
23	24
30	31

*E*very January when I put my new calendar up on the wall, all the empty white squares look so full of promise. I guess spring is when most people think of new beginnings, but I get that feeling of new possibilities each January. One of my resolutions this year is to make a real effort to keep a few more spots on the calendar blank. We all can use a little pampering and downtime now and then, and a visit to a bookstore or a salon can be just the thing for a quick pick-me-up. I find that when I set aside a little time for myself, I'm more effective and cheerful doing the things I'm required to do. So join me in resolving to be just a little lazier this year. Go ahead and pencil in a few "stay in your pajamas" days on your calendar. It's a resolution you'll love to keep!

Hoppin' John Risotto

Hoppin' John Risotto is an Italian take on a traditional Southern dish. It's well known in the South that eating Hoppin' John (a mixture of black-eyed peas and white rice cooked with some type of pork fat) on New Year's Day brings good luck. This dish combines black-eyed peas with Arborio rice, which when cooked with several additions of chicken broth becomes a creamy, full-flavored substitute for the white rice.

Makes 10 to 12 servings

¼   cup butter
½   cup chopped onion
½   cup chopped celery
2   cloves garlic, minced
2   cups Arborio rice
¾   cup white wine
One 15.5-ounce can black-eyed peas, drained and rinsed
One 32-ounce box plus one 14-ounce can chicken broth, warmed
1   teaspoon salt
½   teaspoon crushed red pepper flakes
8   slices bacon, cooked and crumbled
Garnish: chopped fresh parsley and crumbled bacon

In a large saucepan, melt butter over medium heat. Add onion, celery, and garlic, and cook for 5 minutes, or until tender. Stir in rice and cook, stirring frequently, for 5 minutes, or until lightly browned. Stir in wine; cook until wine is absorbed, stirring frequently. Reduce heat to medium low, and stir in black-eyed peas. Add 1 cup warm chicken broth; cook, stirring constantly, until liquid is absorbed. Repeat procedure with remaining chicken broth, 1 cup at a time, allowing liquid to be absorbed after each addition, stirring constantly. Remove from heat and stir in salt, crushed red pepper flakes, and bacon. Garnish with fresh parsley and crumbled bacon, if desired. Serve immediately.

December/January

Tuesday 30

Wednesday 31

Eat your black-eyed peas for good luck and greens for money!

Thursday 1

New Year's Day

Friday 2

Saturday 3

It's National Spaghetti Day. Guess what's for dinner?

Sunday 4

December						
S	M	T	W	T	F	S
	1	2	3	4	5	6
7	8	9	10	11	12	13
14	15	16	17	18	19	20
21	22	23	24	25	26	27
28	29	30	31			

January						
S	M	T	W	T	F	S
				1	2	3
4	5	6	7	8	9	10
11	12	13	14	15	16	17
18	19	20	21	22	23	24
25	26	27	28	29	30	31

Family Message Board

We all try to get more organized in the new year, and this project will get you excited about it. Create a stylish one-of-a-kind bulletin board for your kitchen. Select a favorite fabric, and cover a sheet of corkboard. Then pick a complementary molding at your local framing shop and have them finish the project for you or frame it yourself. Don't let your family miss a beat in their busy lives: post dates and messages on the board for all to see

January

Monday 5

Tuesday 6

Wednesday 7

Thursday 8

The Lady & Sons restaurant turns 13 today!

Friday 9

Saturday 10

Cook a big pot of soup and freeze some for a cold February night.

Sunday 11

January						
S	M	T	W	T	F	S
				1	2	3
4	5	6	7	8	9	10
11	12	13	14	15	16	17
18	19	20	21	22	23	24
25	26	27	28	29	30	31

February						
S	M	T	W	T	F	S
1	2	3	4	5	6	7
8	9	10	11	12	13	14
15	16	17	18	19	20	21
22	23	24	25	26	27	28

Any-Occasion Chicken Pot Pie

This is the perfect recipe to comfort your family on cold days.
The Flaky Pastry Crust really seals the deal.

MAKES 10 TO 12 SERVINGS

3   cups unpeeled red potatoes, cut
    into 1/4-inch cubes
2   cups fresh broccoli florets
1   cup thinly sliced fresh carrots
1/2 cup butter
1   large onion, chopped
1   cup sliced fresh baby portabella
    mushrooms
1/2 cup all-purpose flour
1 1/2 teaspoons dried tarragon leaves
1/2 teaspoon salt
1/4 teaspoon ground black pepper
Two 14.5-ounce cans chicken broth
1   cup heavy whipping cream
3   cups chopped cooked chicken
Flaky Pastry Crust (recipe follows)
1   large egg, lightly beaten

Lightly grease a 3 1/2-quart baking dish.

Place the potatoes in a large saucepan with enough water to cover. Bring to a boil over medium-high heat; boil 5 minutes. Add broccoli and carrots; return to a boil and cook 3 minutes. Drain well and set side.

In a large saucepan, melt butter over medium heat. Add onion and mushrooms and cook 5 minutes, or until tender, stirring occasionally. Stir in flour, tarragon, salt, and pepper, and cook 3 minutes, stirring constantly. Stir in chicken broth and cream, and cook 6 to 8 minutes, or until thickened. Stir in chicken and vegetables, and cook 15 to 20 minutes, or until thickened and bubbly. Pour into prepared baking dish.

Preheat oven to 400°F.

On a lightly floured surface, roll Flaky Pastry Crust to 1/8-inch thickness; cut into 1/2-inch strips. Arrange crust in lattice design over filling; trim strips even with edges of dish. Brush crust with lightly beaten egg. Bake 25 to 30 minutes, or until crust is lightly browned.

Flaky Pastry Crust
MAKES PASTRY FOR 1 CASSEROLE

2 1/4 cups all-purpose flour
1/2 teaspoon salt
1/2 cup cold vegetable shortening,
    diced
1/4 cup cold unsalted butter, diced
1/4 cup cold water

Position knife blade in food processor bowl; add flour and salt, pulsing to combine. Add shortening and butter; pulse until mixture resembles coarse meal. With processor running, add cold water, processing just until combined.

Press mixture gently into a 4-inch disk; cover with heavy-duty plastic wrap, and chill 1 hour.

January

Monday 12

Tuesday 13

Wednesday 14

Thursday 15

Make good use of your time indoors. Clean out a closet or two.

Friday 16

Saturday 17

Sunday 18

January						
S	M	T	W	T	F	S
				1	2	3
4	5	6	7	8	9	10
11	12	13	14	15	16	17
18	19	20	21	22	23	24
25	26	27	28	29	30	31

February						
S	M	T	W	T	F	S
1	2	3	4	5	6	7
8	9	10	11	12	13	14
15	16	17	18	19	20	21
22	23	24	25	26	27	28

The Well-Stocked Pantry

Stocking a pantry is as individual as buying a pair of shoes. The well-stocked pantry of a cook who prepares many meals from scratch is quite different from that of a cook who primarily uses mixes or prepared items. Following are some suggestions for basic items to help you get started.

Basic Pantry

Baking mix or pancake mix
Baking powder
Baking soda
Brownie mix
Canned beef broth or consommé
Canned chicken
Canned chicken broth
Canned corn
Canned fruits
Canned soups
Canned tomatoes
Canned tuna
Canned or dried beans
Chocolate chips
Cocoa
Coffee (instant, ground, or beans)
Condensed milk
Cooked cereals (oatmeal, grits, cream of wheat, etc.)
Cornstarch
Crackers
Dry cereals
Evaporated milk
Flour (all-purpose and self-rising)
Jelly
Ketchup
Mayonnaise
Mustard
Nonstick cooking spray
Olives
Pasta
Peanut butter
Pickles
Popcorn
Red wine vinegar
Rice and rice mixes
Salad dressings
Spaghetti sauce
Sugar (granulated, confectioners', and brown)
Syrup (cane or maple)
Tea bags
Vanilla extract
Vegetable oil
White vinegar
Worcestershire sauce
Yeast (always buy the smallest amount needed)

Basic Herbs

For maximum flavor, write the date on the herb/spice jar when it is purchased, store in a cool place, and discard after one year.

Basil
Bay leaves
Cinnamon
Garlic powder
Nutmeg
Onion powder or flakes
Oregano
Paprika
Pepper (coarse ground and/or whole)
Sage
Salt (iodized and sea salt)
Rosemary
Thyme

January

Monday 19

It's my birthday, y'all!

Martin Luther King Jr. Day

Tuesday 20

Wednesday 21

Thursday 22

Make plans to host a Super Bowl party.

Friday 23

Saturday 24

Sunday 25

January							February						
S	M	T	W	T	F	S	S	M	T	W	T	F	S
				1	2	3	1	2	3	4	5	6	7
4	5	6	7	8	9	10	8	9	10	11	12	13	14
11	12	13	14	15	16	17	15	16	17	18	19	20	21
18	19	20	21	22	23	24	22	23	24	25	26	27	28
25	26	27	28	29	30	31							

Steak Fajita Chili

Peppers, black beans, and tender flank steak give this chili a Southwestern flair.
Great for serving on Super Bowl Sunday.

Makes 10 to 12 servings

One 1-pound flank steak
2 tablespoons vegetable oil
1 red bell pepper, chopped
1 green bell pepper, chopped
1 yellow bell pepper, chopped
2 onions, chopped
2 cups water
Three 15-ounce cans tomato sauce
One 15-ounce can ranch-style beans
One 15-ounce can black beans
One 14.5-ounce can petit diced
    tomatoes
$\frac{1}{4}$ cup chopped fresh cilantro
3 teaspoons ancho chili powder
2 teaspoons ground cumin
2 teaspoons fresh lime juice
1 teaspoon garlic salt

1 teaspoon ground black pepper
Garnish: shredded sharp
    Cheddar cheese, sour cream

Cut steak across grain into thin strips. Cut strips into 1-inch pieces.

In a large Dutch oven, heat oil over medium-high heat. Add steak; cook 5 minutes, stirring frequently. Add pepper and onion; cook 5 minutes. Stir in water, tomato sauce, beans, diced tomatoes, cilantro, chili powder, cumin, lime juice, garlic salt, and pepper. Bring to a boil over medium-high heat; reduce heat and simmer 30 minutes. Garnish with cheese and sour cream, if desired.

January/February

Monday 26

_____
_____
_____
_____

Tuesday 27

Curl up and read a good book.
_____
_____
_____
_____

Wednesday 28

_____
_____
_____
_____

Thursday 29

_____
_____
_____
_____

Friday 30

_____
_____
_____
_____

Saturday 31

_____
_____
_____
_____

Sunday 1

Super Bowl Sunday
_____
_____
_____

January						
S	M	T	W	T	F	S
				1	2	3
4	5	6	7	8	9	10
11	12	13	14	15	16	17
18	19	20	21	22	23	24
25	26	27	28	29	30	31

February						
S	M	T	W	T	F	S
1	2	3	4	5	6	7
8	9	10	11	12	13	14
15	16	17	18	19	20	21
22	23	24	25	26	27	28

February 2009

Sunday	Monday	Tuesday	Wednesday	Thursday
1	2	3	4	5
8	9	10	11	12
15	Presidents' Day 16	17	18	19
22	23	24	Ash Wednesday 25	26

Friday	Saturday
6	7
13	Valentine's Day 14
20	21
27	28

*W*hen I was in grammar school, on Valentine's Day everybody would bring valentines and pass them out to the class. I could hardly wait to see what cards I would get from whom and whether the card hinted that the boy wanted to be my boyfriend, especially if he was a cute one that I had my eye on. It was so exciting!

The uncertainty of Valentine's Day from my past can't hold a flame to celebrating my commitment to my soul mate, best friend, and husband, Michael. He has been such a blessing in my life, and I appreciate him every day. This Valentine's Day, I hope you are aware of how loved you are. And I'm not just talking about romantic love, either. Take a moment to appreciate how rich your life is because of the love of your family and friends. A holiday about love. Now, that's sure worth celebrating!

Chocolate Cheesecakes for Two

Surprise your sweetie on Valentine's Day with a home-cooked meal and these decadent chocolate cheesecakes. You know, chocolate is the quickest way to a man's heart.

MAKES TWO 4-INCH CHEESECAKES

Crust:
½ cup chocolate graham cracker
crumbs
2 tablespoons sugar
2 tablespoons butter, melted

Filling:
2 ounces bittersweet chocolate
1 tablespoon butter
12 ounces cream cheese,
softened
⅓ cup sugar
2 teaspoons Dutch-processed cocoa
powder
1 large egg
1 egg yolk
¼ cup sour cream
1 teaspoon vanilla extract
2 tablespoons heavy whipping cream
2 ounces semisweet chocolate
Garnish: fresh whipped cream, shaved
chocolate, fresh raspberries

Preheat oven to 300°F.

In a small bowl, combine graham cracker crumbs and sugar; add melted butter, stirring well. Press mixture into bottom and up sides of two 4-inch springform pans. Bake 6 minutes; set aside to cool.

In a small microwave-safe bowl, combine bittersweet chocolate and butter. Microwave at high in 30-second intervals, stirring after each, until chocolate is melted and smooth; set aside to cool slightly.

In a medium bowl, beat cream cheese, sugar, and cocoa powder at medium speed with an electric mixer until creamy. Beat in egg and egg yolk, just until combined. Stir in melted chocolate mixture, sour cream, and vanilla. Pour into prepared crusts. Bake 40 minutes; cool completely. Cover and chill 4 hours.

Gently run a knife around edges of pan to release sides. Remove sides from pan.

In a small microwave-safe bowl, combine cream and semisweet chocolate. Microwave at high in 30-second intervals, stirring after each, until chocolate is melted and smooth. Spread evenly over each cheesecake. Garnish with whipped cream, shaved chocolate, and raspberries, if desired.

February

Monday 2

Tuesday 3

Wednesday 4

Thursday 5

National Chocolate Fondue Day

Friday 6

Saturday 7

Sunday 8

Start making travel plans for a spring vacation.

February							March						
S	M	T	W	T	F	S	S	M	T	W	T	F	S
1	2	3	4	5	6	7	1	2	3	4	5	6	7
8	9	10	11	12	13	14	8	9	10	11	12	13	14
15	16	17	18	19	20	21	15	16	17	18	19	20	21
22	23	24	25	26	27	28	22	23	24	25	26	27	28
							29	30	31				

Chocolate Sugar Cookies

Pink icing and pastel sprinkles contrast with chocolate hearts to make a batch of cookies that's prettier than a bouquet of roses. Let the kids help out with decorating so they can share their "art" with classmates at school Valentine's Day parties.

MAKES ABOUT 4 DOZEN COOKIES

1   cup (2 sticks) butter, softened
2   cups sugar
3   large eggs
2   teaspoons vanilla extract
3¼ cups all-purpose flour
¾   cup unsweetened cocoa powder
2   teaspoons baking powder
½   teaspoon salt
Powdered Sugar Icing (recipe follows)
Colored sugar

Powdered Sugar Icing
MAKES ¾ CUP

2   cups confectioners' sugar
¼   cup water
¼   teaspoon vanilla extract
Food coloring (optional)

In a small bowl, whisk together all ingredients. Add food coloring as desired.

Beat butter with an electric mixer on medium speed until soft and creamy; gradually add sugar, beating well. Add eggs and vanilla, beating well.

Combine flour, cocoa, baking powder, and salt; gradually add to butter mixture, mixing well. Cover and chill for 1 hour.

Preheat oven to 350°F. Grease cookie sheets.

Divide dough in half. On a lightly floured surface, roll 1 portion of dough to ⅛-inch thickness. Cut with various sizes of heart-shaped cookie cutters, and place on prepared cookie sheets. Sprinkle with colored sugar, if desired. Repeat procedure with remaining cookie dough, rerolling dough as necessary.

Bake for 10 minutes. Allow to cool for 2 minutes on cookie sheets. Remove to wire racks to cool completely. Once cool, decorate with icing and colored sugar, if desired.

February

Monday 9

Tuesday 10

Wednesday 11

Make cookies for your Valentine.

Thursday 12

Friday 13

Cook a romantic meal for your sweetie.

Saturday 14

Valentine's Day

Sunday 15

February							March						
S	M	T	W	T	F	S	S	M	T	W	T	F	S
1	2	3	4	5	6	7	1	2	3	4	5	6	7
8	9	10	11	12	13	14	8	9	10	11	12	13	14
15	16	17	18	19	20	21	15	16	17	18	19	20	21
22	23	24	25	26	27	28	22	23	24	25	26	27	28
							29	30	31				

User-Friendly Kitchen

A lot of traffic flows through this important room—parents, kids, grandparents, neighbors, guests, and caretakers—so making it user-friendly for everyone is essential. The following strategies will help you organize your kitchen for maximum efficiency.

Schedule a block of time to get daily chores done.
If you don't see a few free hours on the horizon, grab small blocks of "free" time here and there. You'll be surprised how much you can accomplish in five, ten, or fifteen minutes.

Throw away and give away as much as possible.
Be ruthless with things like dilapidated aluminum pans, grocery sacks, and those plastic take-out containers that seem to multiply like rabbits in your cabinets.

Store items close to the place they are used most often.
Instead of thinking, "Where can I store this?" ask yourself, "Where do I use this?" Strive for one-motion storage.

Allocate your most accessible space to the things you use most often.
Shelves between eye and waist level are prime storage areas in your kitchen. So don't store your crêpe pan, which you use infrequently, in front of your saucepans, which you use daily.

Make finding as easy as storing.
Use only clear-glass or plastic containers for storing food in your pantry or refrigerator so you can always keep an eye on what you're saving.

Give every item in the kitchen a home.
When considering buying something new, be it a set of new dishes or a pasta maker, decide where you'll keep it before you bring it home.

Create work centers.
Think of your kitchen in terms of the tasks you perform there (chopping, baking, lunch making, etc.), and arrange the workstations accordingly.

Use organizing tools to maximize space in cabinets and drawers.
- Use plastic bins or sliding wire baskets to store items in the dead space under your sink. (Position bins and baskets so that you can get to shutoff valves easily.)
- Hang a towel rack on the inside of the cabinet door under your sink for storing dishrags and gloves.
- Hang an organizer inside a cabinet or pantry door for aluminum foil, plastic wrap, and bags.
- Use silverware organizers not only for your eating and serving utensils, but also for organizing a junk drawer.
- Use stair-step spice racks to help you see at a glance what you have on hand.
- Use vertical dividers in a lower cabinet close to the oven to store cookie sheets.
- Attach small brochure racks (available at office supply stores) to the inside of cabinet doors for sauces and mixes in small packages.

February

Monday 16

Presidents' Day

Tuesday 17

Wednesday 18

Thursday 19

It's not too early to start preparing your income taxes.

Friday 20

Saturday 21

Sunday 22

February							March						
S	M	T	W	T	F	S	S	M	T	W	T	F	S
1	2	3	4	5	6	7	1	2	3	4	5	6	7
8	9	10	11	12	13	14	8	9	10	11	12	13	14
15	16	17	18	19	20	21	15	16	17	18	19	20	21
22	23	24	25	26	27	28	22	23	24	25	26	27	28
							29	30	31				

Italian Sausage Soup

Full of spicy sausage, tortellini, and vegetables, this hearty soup is a real treat. And the warm Black Olive Scones are perfect for sopping up juices in the bottom of the bowl.

Makes 10 to 12 servings

One 1.24-pound package hot Italian sausage, casings removed
2   carrots, diced
1   onion, chopped
1   green bell pepper, chopped
3   cloves garlic, minced
Two 32-ounce boxes low-sodium chicken broth
One 15-ounce can tomato sauce
2   medium zucchini, cut in half lengthwise and thinly sliced
1   teaspoon dried crushed rosemary
One 20-ounce package refrigerated 3-cheese tortellini
Garnish: chopped fresh parsley

In a large Dutch oven, combine sausage, carrots, onion, bell pepper, and garlic;

cook over medium heat until sausage is browned and crumbles. Drain well.

Stir in chicken broth and tomato sauce; bring to a boil, reduce heat, and simmer 5 minutes. Add zucchini and rosemary; simmer 20 minutes. Add tortellini; simmer 5 minutes, or until tender. Serve immediately. Garnish with chopped fresh parsley, if desired.

Black Olive Scones
Makes about 1 dozen

$2^{1}/_{2}$ cups all-purpose flour
2   tablespoons sugar
2   teaspoons baking powder
$^{1}/_{2}$ teaspoon salt
$^{1}/_{2}$ cup butter
3   tablespoons chopped black olives
$^{2}/_{3}$ cup heavy whipping cream
Olive oil
Kosher salt

Preheat oven to 375°F. Lightly grease a baking sheet.

In a medium bowl, combine flour, sugar, baking powder, and salt. Cut in butter, using a pastry blender, until mixture is crumbly. Stir in olives. Gradually add cream, stirring just until dry ingredients are moistened.

On a lightly floured surface, roll out dough to $^{1}/_{2}$-inch thickness. Cut with a $2^{1}/_{2}$-inch round cutter. Place on prepared baking sheet. Brush with olive oil and sprinkle with salt. Bake 14 to 16 minutes, or until lightly browned. Serve warm.

February/March

Monday 23

Tuesday 24

Happy Mardi Gras! Cook something New Orleans–style tonight.

Wednesday 25

Ash Wednesday

Thursday 26

Friday 27

Saturday 28

Sunday 1

February							March						
S	M	T	W	T	F	S	S	M	T	W	T	F	S
1	2	3	4	5	6	7	1	2	3	4	5	6	7
8	9	10	11	12	13	14	8	9	10	11	12	13	14
15	16	17	18	19	20	21	15	16	17	18	19	20	21
22	23	24	25	26	27	28	22	23	24	25	26	27	28
							29	30	31				

March 2009

Sunday	Monday	Tuesday	Wednesday	Thursday
1	2	3	4	5
8	9	10	11	12
15	16	St. Patrick's Day 17	18	19
22	23	24	25	26
29	30	31		

Friday	Saturday
6	7
13	14
20	21
27	28

I can't believe that spring is almost here. Not that I'm complaining. I absolutely love the spring—it's one of my favorite times of the year. The summer heat hasn't set in yet, the flowers are coming up, and everything just feels reborn. When I get spring fever, I want to go fishing or work in the garden or just do anything, as long as it's outside. It's such a relief to get outdoors after being cooped up all winter. I open the windows wide and let the fresh air in. It's just a wonderful feeling.

The folks in Savannah love this time of year, especially St. Patrick's Day. We have the second-largest celebration in the country—the city really pulls out the stops. At The Lady & Sons, we get in the spirit, too. In the past, we've served a breakfast of green grits and put corned beef and cabbage on the buffet. It's so much fun. So happy spring and happy St. Patrick's Day, y'all!

Salmon Burgers with Asian Aioli

When the weather begins to warm, I can't wait to get outside and grill. These Salmon Burgers are fun to make and prove to be a nice variation of the all-American favorite.

Makes 8 servings

½ cup minced red bell pepper
½ cup minced yellow bell pepper
½ cup panko (Japanese bread crumbs)
2 cloves garlic, minced
2 pounds salmon fillets, skinned and finely chopped
1 large egg, lightly beaten
1 tablespoon soy sauce
½ teaspoon fresh lemon juice
½ teaspoon salt
Asian Aioli (recipe follows)
8 buttered and toasted sandwich buns
8 lettuce leaves

Asian Aioli
Makes about 1 cup

1 cup mayonnaise
2 cloves garlic, minced
1 teaspoon soy sauce
½ teaspoon sesame oil

In a small bowl, combine all the ingredients. Cover and chill.

In a medium bowl, combine peppers, panko, garlic, and salmon.

In a small bowl, combine egg, soy sauce, lemon juice, and salt; add to pepper mixture, tossing gently to combine. Form mixture into 8 patties.

Lightly coat a grill pan or skillet with cooking spray. Heat over medium-high heat until hot. Grill or cook patties, 5 minutes per side, or until desired degree of doneness.

Spread Asian Aioli evenly over both halves of the toasted buns; top each with lettuce leaf and salmon patty. Cover with tops of buns.

March

Monday 2

Tuesday 3

Wednesday 4

Thursday 5

Friday 6

It's our wedding anniversary!

Saturday 7

Sunday 8

Daylight savings time begins

March						
S	M	T	W	T	F	S
1	2	3	4	5	6	7
8	9	10	11	12	13	14
15	16	17	18	19	20	21
22	23	24	25	26	27	28
29	30	31				

April						
S	M	T	W	T	F	S
			1	2	3	4
5	6	7	8	9	10	11
12	13	14	15	16	17	18
19	20	21	22	23	24	25
26	27	28	29	30		

Start Thinking About Your Herb Garden

Now is the time to start ordering seeds and laying out plans for your garden. Herbs are a favorite of mine because you can grow them in the ground, in pots, or on a windowsill. Here are two suggestions for tasty herbs to grow.

Parsley

There are two common types of parsley: curly leaf and flat leaf (or Italian). The attractive curly leaf is generally used as a garnish. Flat leaf is often used in cooking because of its stronger flavor. Parsley is thought to have gained popularity when Catherine de Médicis brought the herb with her from its native Italy to France. As far back as the days of Hippocrates, it was used for multiple medical purposes. Though scientific research has found the herb to have some medicinal uses, it is more often used as a garnish or as an ingredient in Middle Eastern, European, and American cooking. If you're at a restaurant and suspect you may have bad breath, discreetly gnaw on a piece of your garnish. The heavy concentration of chlorophyll in parsley makes it a surprisingly effective breath freshener.

Rosemary

Traditionally rosemary was an emblem of fidelity for lovers. Rosemary's name is rooted in folklore. It is said that the Virgin Mary draped her cloak over a bush and placed a white flower on the top of the cloak. In the morning, the flower had turned blue, and thereafter the plant was called Rose of Mary. The fragrant, woody evergreen is fairly easy to grow, and since it is drought-resistant, it is often used in landscaping. The silver-green, spiky leaves are a very popular culinary spice, pairing well with pork, fish, chicken, and especially lamb. In addition to keeping rosemary in my garden, I keep some by the back door because the smell is just heavenly!

Did You Know?

In ancient times, herbs were valued for their healing powers, but these days they are more likely to be used to dress up a garden or spice up a kitchen. The herbs in my garden spend a little time looking pretty growing in my backyard, and then I snip them, dry them, and use them in my cooking. Store-bought herbs just can't compare with fresh herbs from the garden.

March

Monday 9

Tuesday 10

Wednesday 11

Thursday 12

Plan a fix-it-and-forget-it meal for this weekend.

Friday 13

Saturday 14

Sunday 15

March							April						
S	M	T	W	T	F	S	S	M	T	W	T	F	S
1	2	3	4	5	6	7				1	2	3	4
8	9	10	11	12	13	14	5	6	7	8	9	10	11
15	16	17	18	19	20	21	12	13	14	15	16	17	18
22	23	24	25	26	27	28	19	20	21	22	23	24	25
29	30	31					26	27	28	29	30		

Pecan Chicken Salad

Everyone's recipe repertoire should include a good chicken salad, and this one is tasty and easy to make. It will be at home at a ladies' luncheon, baby shower, or bridal shower. For a meal with more substance, pair it with buttery croissants to make a yummy sandwich.

MAKES 4 TO 6 SERVINGS

$^1/_2$ cup mayonnaise
$^1/_4$ cup sour cream
3   cups chopped cooked chicken
1   cup seedless grapes, halved
$^3/_4$ cup toasted chopped pecans
Salt and pepper

In a medium bowl, combine mayonnaise and sour cream. Stir in chicken, grapes, and pecans. Add salt and pepper to taste.

March

Monday 16

Tuesday 17

Be sure to wear green today!

St. Patrick's Day

Wednesday 18

Thursday 19

Friday 20

First Day of Spring

Saturday 21

Sunday 22

		March							April			
S	M	T	W	T	F	S	S	M	T	W	T	F	S
	1	2	3	4	5	6	7				1	2	3	4
8	9	10	11	12	13	14	5	6	7	8	9	10	11
15	16	17	18	19	20	21	12	13	14	15	16	17	18
22	23	24	25	26	27	28	19	20	21	22	23	24	25
29	30	31					26	27	28	29	30		

Grits Pie

I do love grits, and thanks to this pie, I can have them for dessert.
With the consistency of custard and a delicate sweetness, this dish will make you
wonder why you've always eaten them for breakfast.

MAKES ONE 9-INCH PIE

$3/4$ cup water
$1/8$ teaspoon salt
$1/4$ cup quick-cooking grits
$1/2$ cup (1 stick) butter
$3/4$ cup sugar
2   tablespoons all-purpose flour
3   large eggs, slightly beaten
$1/4$ cup buttermilk
1   teaspoon vanilla extract
One 9-inch frozen pie shell, thawed and
    unbaked
Garnish: sweetened whipped cream
    and strawberries

Preheat oven to 325°F.

In a small saucepan, bring water and salt to a boil. Add grits and cook for 4 minutes, stirring constantly. Add butter and cook for an additional minute. Set aside and cool slightly.

In a small bowl, stir together sugar, flour, eggs, buttermilk, and vanilla. Stir into cooked grits. Pour into pie shell and bake for 35 to 40 minutes, or until set. Serve warm or cold with whipped cream and strawberries as a garnish, if desired.

March

Monday 23

Tuesday 24

Get ready to plant spring flowers by cleaning out beds.   **Wednesday 25**

Thursday 26

Friday 27

Saturday 28

Sunday 29

		March							April				
S	M	T	W	T	F	S	S	M	T	W	T	F	S
1	2	3	4	5	6	7				1	2	3	4
8	9	10	11	12	13	14	5	6	7	8	9	10	11
15	16	17	18	19	20	21	12	13	14	15	16	17	18
22	23	24	25	26	27	28	19	20	21	22	23	24	25
29	30	31					26	27	28	29	30		

Spring

It's time to celebrate new
beginnings, warm air, and the sweet
flavors of the season.

April 2009

Sunday	Monday	Tuesday	Wednesday	Thursday
			April Fool's Day 1	2
Palm Sunday 5	6	7	8	Passover begins 9
Easter 12	13	14	15	16
19	20	21	Earth Day 22	23
26	27	28	29	30

Friday	Saturday
3	4
Good Friday 10	11
17	18
24	25

I've always enjoyed Easter so much. When I was a girl, it was my Aunt Peggy who made a basket for me. When I was a young mother, she taught me how to put together beautiful Easter baskets. It was great to pass on Easter traditions to my children. Each year, we would dye eggs and have Easter egg hunts in the yard. On Easter morning, I would dress the boys up in their Easter finery, and we would go to the sunrise church service. After that, we'd go out for breakfast. It sure was a full morning.

But those baskets! I would just stuff them full of goodies and then tie it all up with a ribbon. Those baskets were so jam-packed you couldn't see half of what was in there.

I really don't have a traditional Easter meal that I make each year. It's pretty wide open except that the main dish has got to be ham. That's probably because my mother always served it. All I know is, it's just not Easter without that ham in the center of the table and beautiful baskets filled with goodies.

Chicken Piccata Stuffed Mushrooms

Serve these stuffed mushrooms at your next party. They're great pick-up appetizers and can be made ahead of time. Make plenty, though, because it's hard to eat just one.

MAKES ABOUT 2½ DOZEN

2 pounds fresh button mushrooms
6 tablespoons butter
¼ cup minced green onion
1 tablespoon minced capers
1 teaspoon dried thyme
½ teaspoon salt
¼ teaspoon ground black pepper
1 cup chopped cooked chicken
½ cup dry white wine
4 ounces cream cheese
½ cup panko (Japanese bread crumbs)
¼ cup butter, melted

Preheat oven to 350°F. Grease a 15 x 10-inch jelly-roll pan.

Clean mushrooms, removing stems; set caps aside. Finely chop enough mushroom stems to equal ½ cup. Discard remaining stems.

In a large skillet, melt 6 tablespoons butter over medium heat. Add mushroom stems, green onion, capers, thyme, salt, and pepper; cook 5 minutes, stirring frequently, or until the stems are tender. Stir in chicken and wine; cook 5 minutes, or until wine has evaporated. Add cream cheese and panko, stirring until combined.

Fill mushroom caps evenly with chicken mixture. Place in pan, and brush each with melted butter. Bake 20 minutes. Serve immediately.

Note: Mushroom caps may be filled 2 days before baking. Cover with plastic wrap and refrigerate until ready to bake.

March/April

Monday 30

Tuesday 31

Wednesday 1

April Fool's Day

Thursday 2

Start planning for Easter lunch and Easter baskets.

Friday 3

Saturday 4

Sunday 5

Palm Sunday

March							April						
S	M	T	W	T	F	S	S	M	T	W	T	F	S
1	2	3	4	5	6	7				1	2	3	4
8	9	10	11	12	13	14	5	6	7	8	9	10	11
15	16	17	18	19	20	21	12	13	14	15	16	17	18
22	23	24	25	26	27	28	19	20	21	22	23	24	25
29	30	31					26	27	28	29	30		

Veggie Pasta Salad

This cool, crisp salad is the perfect side to take to a picnic, and it's a great make-ahead dish.

Makes 8 servings

3   carrots, cut in ¼-inch julienne
1   red bell pepper, cut in
    ¼-inch julienne
2   cups fresh broccoli florets
1   cup halved grape tomatoes
One 2.25-ounce can sliced black olives,
    drained
8   ounces ziti, cooked
⅔   cup olive oil
2   tablespoons fresh lemon juice
2   tablespoons Dijon mustard
1   teaspoon dried parsley
1   teaspoon dried basil
1   teaspoon dried oregano
½   teaspoon salt
½   teaspoon ground black pepper
Garnish: fresh basil

In a large bowl, combine carrots, bell pepper, broccoli, tomatoes, olives, and ziti.

In a small bowl, whisk together oil, lemon juice, mustard, parsley, basil, oregano, salt, and black pepper. Pour over carrot mixture, tossing gently to coat. Cover and chill 2 hours. Garnish with fresh basil, if desired.

April

Monday 6

Tuesday 7

Wednesday 8

Thursday 9

Passover begins at sundown

Friday 10

It's time to dye Easter eggs with the little ones. Use the eggs to decorate your holiday table.

Good Friday

Saturday 11

Sunday 12

Easter

April							May						
S	M	T	W	T	F	S	S	M	T	W	T	F	S
			1	2	3	4						1	2
5	6	7	8	9	10	11	3	4	5	6	7	8	9
12	13	14	15	16	17	18	10	11	12	13	14	15	16
19	20	21	22	23	24	25	17	18	19	20	21	22	23
26	27	28	29	30			24	25	26	27	28	29	30
							31						

Spring Break

With things warming up, I've been getting nostalgic for spring break. When I was growing up in Albany, we'd all go down to Panama City, Florida. I wasn't allowed until I was a senior in high school, and let me tell you, when I finally got to go, I had the best time. I would dance on the boardwalk, run up and down the strip, see all my friends, and just party. It was great.

When my boys were teenagers, my husband and I, along with another couple, would chaperone a group of kids there, and we just had a ball. We knew we had to keep our eyes on the kids (they were as slippery as eels), but I really looked forward to having that time with my boys. It was such a joy to watch them having fun like I did when I was their age.

If you're traveling with your family this spring, enjoy every second.

April

Monday 13

National Peach Cobbler Day

Tuesday 14

Wednesday 15

Income taxes due!

Thursday 16

Friday 17

Saturday 18

Sunday 19

April								May					
S	M	T	W	T	F	S		S	M	T	W	T	F	S
			1	2	3	4							1	2
5	6	7	8	9	10	11		3	4	5	6	7	8	9
12	13	14	15	16	17	18		10	11	12	13	14	15	16
19	20	21	22	23	24	25		17	18	19	20	21	22	23
26	27	28	29	30				24	25	26	27	28	29	30
								31						

S'mores Cake

A grown-up version of a kid-friendly treat—we always want "some more."

MAKES 10 TO 12 SERVINGS

One 18.25-ounce package chocolate
   cake mix with pudding
1¼ cups graham cracker crumbs
1¼ cups water
⅓ cup vegetable oil
3 large eggs
Marshmallow Cream Frosting
   (recipe follows)
Garnish: graham cracker crumbs and
   strawberries

Preheat oven to 350°F. Grease and flour a 13 x 9-inch baking pan.

In a large bowl, combine cake mix, cracker crumbs, water, oil, and eggs. Beat at medium speed with an electric mixer until smooth. Spoon into prepared pan. Bake 30 minutes, or until a wooden pick inserted in center comes out clean. Cool completely.

Spread Marshmallow Cream Frosting evenly over cake. Sprinkle with graham cracker crumbs and top with strawberries, if desired.

Marshmallow Cream Frosting
MAKES ABOUT 3 CUPS

One 7-ounce jar marshmallow cream
½ cup butter, softened
3½ cups confectioners' sugar
2 tablespoons milk
1 teaspoon vanilla extract

In a medium bowl, beat marshmallow cream and butter at medium speed with an electric mixer until smooth. Gradually beat in confectioners' sugar until smooth. Beat in milk and vanilla.

Monday 20

Tuesday 21

Vow to do something "green" today and every day.

Wednesday 22

Earth Day

Thursday 23

Friday 24

Saturday 25

Sunday 26

April						
S	M	T	W	T	F	S
			1	2	3	4
5	6	7	8	9	10	11
12	13	14	15	16	17	18
19	20	21	22	23	24	25
26	27	28	29	30		

May						
S	M	T	W	T	F	S
					1	2
3	4	5	6	7	8	9
10	11	12	13	14	15	16
17	18	19	20	21	22	23
24	25	26	27	28	29	30
31						

Raspberry Streusel Muffins

If you're having overnight guests, start the morning off right. They'll be delighted to wake up to these irresistible muffins. The Streusel Topping makes them extra good.

Makes 15 muffins

$^1/_2$ cup (1 stick) butter, softened
1 cup sugar
2 large eggs
1 teaspoon vanilla extract
$^1/_2$ teaspoon almond extract
2 cups all-purpose flour
3 teaspoons baking powder
$^1/_4$ teaspoon salt
1 cup milk
1 pint fresh raspberries
Streusel Topping (recipe follows)

Preheat oven to 400°F. Lightly grease 2 muffin pans.

In a medium bowl, beat butter with an electric mixer until creamy. Gradually add sugar, beating until fluffy. Add eggs and extracts, beating until blended.

In a small bowl, combine flour, baking powder, and salt. Add flour mixture to butter mixture alternately with milk, beginning and ending with flour mixture. After each addition, beat at low speed just until blended. Fold in raspberries. Spoon batter into the greased muffin pans, filling three-fourths full. Sprinkle evenly with Streusel Topping.

Bake 20 minutes, or until golden brown. Remove from pans immediately.

Streusel Topping
Makes about 1 cup

$^1/_2$ cup sugar
$^1/_3$ cup all-purpose flour
$^1/_4$ cup ($^1/_2$ stick) butter, softened

In a small bowl, combine sugar and flour. Cut in butter, using a pastry blender, until mixture is crumbly.

Monday 27

Tuesday 28

Wednesday 29

Thursday 30

Buy gifts and cards for the soon-to-be graduates in your life.

Friday 1

Saturday 2

Sunday 3

April							May						
S	M	T	W	T	F	S	S	M	T	W	T	F	S
			1	2	3	4						1	2
5	6	7	8	9	10	11	3	4	5	6	7	8	9
12	13	14	15	16	17	18	10	11	12	13	14	15	16
19	20	21	22	23	24	25	17	18	19	20	21	22	23
26	27	28	29	30			24	25	26	27	28	29	30
							31						

May 2009

Sunday	Monday	Tuesday	Wednesday	Thursday
3	4	Cinco de Mayo 5	6	7
Mother's Day 10	11	12	13	14
17	18	19	20	21
24 31	Memorial Day 25	26	27	28

Friday	Saturday
1	2
8	9
15	16
22	23
29	30

*W*hether it's the baby birds in a nest on the porch, bursting buds in the garden, or simply the mercury rising in the thermometer on the window, spring is such an invigorating time of year. It gets me so energized. With the warm weather and sunshine, I'm ready to play. I just want to take off my shoes and run around in the yard.

Lucky for me, running around in the yard is an old habit for my family. It's how we celebrate birthdays and holidays! At first, all these grown-up children were reluctant to be silly, when I broke out the lawn games, everyone got into the spirit. Now we all look forward to every warm-weather celebration. It's the perfect time of year to find excuses for barbecues, picnics, and lunch dates on the patio with best friends and family. Savor those sweet spring memories. I know I still do, even after all these years!

Mother's Day

I have been so blessed to be a mother. My sons have always been my proudest accomplishment. They are two polite Southern boys, and I am forever indebted to them for the support they gave me when I started my business. During my Bag Lady days, they were my delivery boys, and throughout the many incarnations of the restaurant, they have always been there for me. Now, I know you ladies don't mind when they show their handsome faces on my show! I've loved babying my boys, but I'm proud that I was able to give them wings. They are as loyal and sweet as can be, but they can stand on their own two feet, too.

Do something special for your mother, because I bet you're the apple of your mother's eye, and she deserves your attention.

May

Monday 4

Tuesday 5

Invite the girls over for a Mexican feast.

Cinco de Mayo

Wednesday 6

Thursday 7

Friday 8

Saturday 9

Sunday 10

Mother's Day

May							June					
S	M	T	W	T	F	S	S	M	T	W	T	F	S
					1	2		1	2	3	4	5	6
3	4	5	6	7	8	9	7	8	9	10	11	12	13
10	11	12	13	14	15	16	14	15	16	17	18	19	20
17	18	19	20	21	22	23	21	22	23	24	25	26	27
24	25	26	27	28	29	30	28	29	30				
31												

Crab Cakes with Lemon Dill Sauce

*These crab cakes are full of delicate crabmeat, and the Lemon Dill Sauce
really brings out their fresh taste.*

3   tablespoons butter, divided
1   green onion, finely chopped
2   tablespoons finely chopped red bell
    pepper
1   clove garlic, minced
3   tablespoons heavy cream
1   tablespoon Dijon mustard
Cayenne pepper
1   cup bread crumbs, divided
1   large egg
$^1/_2$ teaspoon minced fresh
    parsley
1   pound white or claw crabmeat, picked
    free of any bits of shell
$^1/_4$ cup grated Parmesan cheese
2   tablespoons vegetable oil
Lemon Dill Sauce (recipe follows)

Melt 1 tablespoon butter in a heavy skillet over medium heat. Add onion, bell pepper, and garlic and cook 3 minutes. Add cream, mustard, and cayenne to taste, and mix well. Add $^1/_2$ cup bread crumbs, egg, and parsley, mixing well. Gently fold in crabmeat.

Form mixture into eight $^1/_2$-inch-thick patties. Combine remaining $^1/_2$ cup bread crumbs and Parmesan in a bowl; pat this topping onto both sides of patties. Refrigerate until firm, about 2 hours.

Combine oil and remaining 2 tablespoons butter in skillet. Cook crab cakes over medium heat for about 3 minutes per side, or until golden brown. Or place them on a baking sheet, drizzle with oil-and-butter mixture, and bake at 400°F for 7 to 10 minutes, turning once.

Spoon a dollop of Lemon Dill Sauce alongside each crab cake, and serve remaining sauce separately.

Lemon Dill Sauce
MAKES ABOUT 1$^1/_2$ CUPS

1   cup mayonnaise
$^1/_4$ cup buttermilk
2   tablespoons chopped fresh dill
1   tablespoon minced fresh parsley
1   tablespoon grated lemon zest
2   teaspoons fresh lemon juice
1   small garlic clove, minced

In a small bowl, combine all ingredients; stir well. Refrigerate until chilled; the sauce will thicken as it chills.

May

Monday 11

Tuesday 12

Wednesday 13

Thursday 14

Friday 15

Saturday 16

Stay in your pajamas all day!

Sunday 17

	May							June					
S	M	T	W	T	F	S	S	M	T	W	T	F	S
					1	2		1	2	3	4	5	6
3	4	5	6	7	8	9	7	8	9	10	11	12	13
10	11	12	13	14	15	16	14	15	16	17	18	19	20
17	18	19	20	21	22	23	21	22	23	24	25	26	27
24	25	26	27	28	29	30	28	29	30				
31													

Tomato Mozzarella Salad

In and around Savannah, the tomatoes are starting to ripen on the vine, and this simple salad is the perfect way to celebrate the beginning of love-apple season.

Makes 4 to 6 servings

4   medium tomatoes, sliced
Fresh basil leaves
$^1/_2$ pound fresh mozzarella cheese,
     thinly sliced
$^1/_2$ teaspoon salt
$^1/_4$ teaspoon freshly ground black pepper
Olive oil
Balsamic vinegar

On a serving plate, alternate tomato slices, fresh basil, and cheese. Sprinkle with salt and pepper. Just prior to serving, drizzle olive oil and balsamic vinegar over tomatoes.

May

Monday 18

Tuesday 19

Wednesday 20

Thursday 21

Friday 22

Saturday 23

Summer's almost here. Clean the patio and get ready for outdoor entertaining.

Sunday 24

	May							June					
S	M	T	W	T	F	S	S	M	T	W	T	F	S
					1	2		1	2	3	4	5	6
3	4	5	6	7	8	9	7	8	9	10	11	12	13
10	11	12	13	14	15	16	14	15	16	17	18	19	20
17	18	19	20	21	22	23	21	22	23	24	25	26	27
24	25	26	27	28	29	30	28	29	30				
31													

Key Lime Ice Cream Pie

Cool and refreshing, this ice cream pie is a great way to end a backyard barbecue.

MAKES ONE 10-INCH PIE

2 cups graham cracker crumbs
¼ cup firmly packed brown sugar
½ cup butter, melted
Key Lime Ice Cream, softened
  (recipe follows)
Garnish: fresh lime slices

Key Lime Ice Cream

2 cups heavy whipping cream
½ cup sugar
Two 14-ounce cans sweetened
  condensed milk
1¼ cups key lime juice
1 tablespoon key lime zest
1 quart half-and-half

Preheat oven to 350°F.

In a medium bowl, combine cracker crumbs and brown sugar. Stir in butter. Press mixture firmly into bottom and sides of a 10-inch springform pan. Bake for 8 minutes; let cool completely. Gently spread softened ice cream over crust. Cover and freeze for 4 hours, or until firm. Cut into wedges to serve. Garnish with fresh lime slices, if desired.

In a large bowl, beat cream at medium speed with an electric mixer until slightly thickened. Gradually add sugar, beating until soft peaks form. Add condensed milk and beat until stiff peaks form. Beat in lime juice, lime zest, and half-and-half.

Pour mixture into freezer container of a 1-gallon electric ice cream maker, and freeze according to manufacturer's instructions. If a firmer texture is desired, transfer ice cream to airtight container and freeze for 2 hours, or until firm.

Get out the grill and invite friends and family over for a feast.

Monday 25

Memorial Day

Tuesday 26

Wednesday 27

Thursday 28

Friday 29

Saturday 30

Sunday 31

		May							June			
S	M	T	W	T	F	S	S	M	T	W	T	F	S
					1	2		1	2	3	4	5	6
3	4	5	6	7	8	9	7	8	9	10	11	12	13
10	11	12	13	14	15	16	14	15	16	17	18	19	20
17	18	19	20	21	22	23	21	22	23	24	25	26	27
24	25	26	27	28	29	30	28	29	30				
31													

June 2009

Sunday	Monday	Tuesday	Wednesday	Thursday
	1	2	3	4
7	8	9	10	11
Flag Day 14	15	16	17	18
Father's Day 21	22	23	24	25
28	29	30		

Friday	Saturday
5	6
12	13
19	20
26	27

*T*he wedding season reaches its peak this month! Now, I didn't get married in the summer because it's too hot in Savannah. But many of you will attend those love-filled events this month, and they always remind me of our special day.

Our wedding day was perfect—everything a girl could dream of. The wedding was in the gorgeous Whitefield Chapel in Savannah. It was truly beautiful. Most important, I was finally married to my answered prayer!

We had a big party with friends and family after the intimate ceremony. Six hundred guests joined us at The Lady and Sons, and we had a ball dancing—and eating—till the wee hours! I remember having just as much fun when Brooke and Jamie were married. They had a fairy-tale wedding and reception, and I loved seeing their dreams come true like they did for Michael and me.

Remember that weddings are joyous events, so put on your dancing shoes and celebrate!

Tomato Sandwiches

There is almost nothing a Southerner likes better than a tomato sandwich. There is an art to a perfect tomato sandwich: vine-ripened tomatoes that have been peeled and sliced and drained overnight on paper towels, day-old white bread, and mayonnaise with seasoned salt. If your tomatoes aren't ripe, don't serve them!
This recipe makes 10 large sandwiches. The bread will go further if the tomatoes are smaller, like Romas, as you can get two rounds out of one slice of bread.

MAKES ABOUT 10 SANDWICHES

2   vine-ripened or Roma tomatoes, thinly sliced
1   loaf day-old thin-sliced white bread
$^{1}/_{2}$ cup mayonnaise
1   teaspoon seasoned salt
Garnish: fresh parsley

Line a baking sheet with paper towels. Place sliced tomatoes in a single layer on paper towels. Allow to drain for several hours or overnight in the refrigerator.

Cut bread into rounds with a biscuit cutter the size of the largest tomato slices. In a small bowl, stir together mayonnaise and seasoned salt.

An hour before serving, spread mayonnaise on bread rounds. Top half of rounds with a tomato slice; cover with another bread round. Garnish with fresh parsley, if desired.

June

Monday 1

Tuesday 2

Wednesday 3

Thursday 4

Friday 5

Saturday 6

Buy Father's Day gifts and cards.

Sunday 7

	June							July					
S	M	T	W	T	F	S	S	M	T	W	T	F	S
	1	2	3	4	5	6				1	2	3	4
7	8	9	10	11	12	13	5	6	7	8	9	10	11
14	15	16	17	18	19	20	12	13	14	15	16	17	18
21	22	23	24	25	26	27	19	20	21	22	23	24	25
28	29	30					26	27	28	29	30	31	

Sunflower Arrangement

For a Mexican fiesta on the veranda, we created this wonderful centerpiece using fresh bell peppers and cut flowers from the market.

The bell peppers are trimmed to make simple vases. They don't require much cleaning and are ready in a flash. I selected several colorful peppers as well as a number of bright flowers.

At home, I quickly put together the centerpiece. I placed two peppers on a small cake stand to add height to the arrangement. Once I placed the other peppers, I surrounded the arrangement with sunflowers. I also placed a few large split-leaf philodendron leaves underneath the peppers and sunflowers. I think it's an easy and adorable way to add flair to the table setting and perfectly festive for any kind of celebration.

June

Monday 8

Tuesday 9

Wednesday 10

Thursday 11

Friday 12

Saturday 13

Fly your flag with pride!

Sunday 14

Flag Day

June							July						
S	M	T	W	T	F	S	S	M	T	W	T	F	S
	1	2	3	4	5	6				1	2	3	4
7	8	9	10	11	12	13	5	6	7	8	9	10	11
14	15	16	17	18	19	20	12	13	14	15	16	17	18
21	22	23	24	25	26	27	19	20	21	22	23	24	25
28	29	30					26	27	28	29	30	31	

Orange Cherry Limeade

Cool and refreshing, this drink is perfect to quench a hot-summer thirst.

MAKES 4 SERVINGS

2   cups Florida's Natural
    orange juice
2   cups prepared limeade
$1/4$ cup grenadine
Garnish: maraschino cherries
    and fresh orange slices

In a small pitcher, combine all ingredients. Serve over ice. Garnish with maraschino cherries and fresh orange slices, if desired.

Mixed Berry Bellinis

For a welcome change, serve your guests richly colored Mixed Berry Bellinis in footed glasses instead of from the usual punch bowl.

MAKES 6 TO 8 SERVINGS

One 12-ounce package frozen mixed
    berries, thawed
$1/4$ cup sugar
One 750-ml bottle sparkling wine

In the container of an electric blender, combine berries and sugar; process until smooth. Strain mixture, if desired. Pour into a serving pitcher; slowly add wine, stirring gently.

June

Monday 15

Tuesday 16

Wednesday 17

Thursday 18

Friday 19

The Bag Lady opened on this day in 1989.

Saturday 20

Sunday 21

First Day of Summer

Father's Day

	June							July					
S	M	T	W	T	F	S	S	M	T	W	T	F	S
	1	2	3	4	5	6				1	2	3	4
7	8	9	10	11	12	13	5	6	7	8	9	10	11
14	15	16	17	18	19	20	12	13	14	15	16	17	18
21	22	23	24	25	26	27	19	20	21	22	23	24	25
28	29	30					26	27	28	29	30	31	

Amaretto Peach Parfaits

This dessert was made to enhance the flavor of sweet Georgia peaches. Crumbled homemade meringues really make it extraordinary.

Makes 6 servings

4   egg whites, at room temperature
1/2 teaspoon cream of tartar
1 1/4 cup sugar, divided
5   ripe peaches, peeled and thinly sliced
1   tablespoon almond-flavored liqueur
Amaretto Cream (recipe follows)
Garnish: chopped almonds and
      crumbled meringues

Preheat oven to 250°F. Line a baking sheet with parchment paper; set aside.

In a large bowl, beat egg whites and cream of tartar at medium-high speed with an electric mixer until foamy. With mixer running, gradually add 1 cup sugar, 1 tablespoon at a time, and beat until stiff peaks form.

Spoon egg-white mixture by tablespoonfuls onto prepared baking sheet. Bake for 1 hour. Turn oven off, and leave meringues in the oven for 8 hours (do not open oven door). Crumble meringues and set aside.

In a medium bowl, combine peaches, 1/4 cup sugar, and almond-flavored liqueur; cover and refrigerate for at least 30 minutes.

Sprinkle 2 tablespoons crumbled meringues into bottoms of each serving dish. Top evenly with Amaretto Cream. Spoon half of peach mixture over each. Repeat procedure with remaining meringues, cream, and peaches. Garnish with chopped almonds and crumbled meringues, if desired.

Amaretto Cream
Makes about 3 1/2 cups

2   cups heavy whipping cream
4   ounces cream cheese, softened
1   cup confectioners' sugar
1/4 cup almond-flavored liqueur

In a medium bowl, combine cream and cream cheese. Beat at medium-high speed with an electric mixer until thickened. Gradually beat in confectioners' sugar, beating until soft peaks form. Beat in liqueur. Cover and refrigerate at least 2 hours, up to 24 hours.

National Onion Rings Day

Monday 22

Tuesday 23

Visit a local farmers' market and enjoy all the season has to offer.

Wednesday 24

Thursday 25

Friday 26

Saturday 27

Sunday 28

		June							July			
S	M	T	W	T	F	S	S	M	T	W	T	F	S
	1	2	3	4	5	6				1	2	3	4
7	8	9	10	11	12	13	5	6	7	8	9	10	11
14	15	16	17	18	19	20	12	13	14	15	16	17	18
21	22	23	24	25	26	27	19	20	21	22	23	24	25
28	29	30					26	27	28	29	30	31	

Summer

Everything tastes better in
summer—tomatoes, peaches,
fresh green beans and peas,
and, of course, cool desserts like
homemade ice cream.

July 2009

Sunday	Monday	Tuesday	Wednesday	Thursday
			1	2
5	6	7	8	9
12	13	14	15	16
19	20	21	22	23
26	27	28	29	30

Friday	Saturday
3	Independence Day 4
10	11
17	18
24	25
31	

*T*he Fourth of July is such a wonderful holiday. There's none of the stress that comes with buying presents for Christmas or the formality of Thanksgiving. It's just a laid-back day filled with food, family, and fun. My family really loves to spend the day on the water, playing on the boat or the Jet Skis. It can get really hot, but on a sunny day, with the breeze coming off the water, you forget about the heat. Of course, if the kids have taken the boat and given the "keep-away" orders, I can have just as much fun in the backyard. Michael throws some meat on the grill, and we play a little croquet. For me, it's a day that I've just got to be outdoors.

Eventually the heat wears off as the sun goes down, and it's time to watch the fireworks. It's so magical to look up and see all the colors against a dark night sky. Sitting on a blanket and enjoying all that beauty truly makes me feel patriotic. Speaking of freedom . . . raise Old Glory and be thankful for our beautiful country!

Pork Ribs with Sweet Pepper Dry Rub

No Independence Day cookout is complete without a grill full of barbecued ribs. The dry rub used in this recipe adds a wonderful depth of flavor. You'll have fireworks going off in your mouth.

MAKES 4 TO 6 SERVINGS

$^1\!/_2$ cup firmly packed brown sugar
$^1\!/_4$ cup sweet paprika
2 tablespoons chili powder
$1^1\!/_2$ tablespoons celery salt
1 tablespoon garlic powder
1 tablespoon onion powder
1 tablespoon salt
$2^1\!/_2$ teaspoons ground black pepper
2 teaspoons dry mustard
1 teaspoon ground thyme
$2^1\!/_2$ pounds St. Louis–cut pork spare ribs

In a medium bowl, combine all the dry ingredients. Rub spare ribs with seasonings until well coated.

Preheat oven to 250°F.

Wrap ribs in 2 layers of heavy-duty aluminum foil. Bake 2 hours. Remove from oven and unwrap. Grill, over medium-high heat, 30 minutes, or until desired degree of tenderness.

June/July

Monday 29

Tuesday 30

Wednesday 1

Thursday 2

Friday 3

Saturday 4

Watch the fireworks with your family and friends.

Independence Day

Sunday 5

June							July						
S	M	T	W	T	F	S	S	M	T	W	T	F	S
	1	2	3	4	5	6				1	2	3	4
7	8	9	10	11	12	13	5	6	7	8	9	10	11
14	15	16	17	18	19	20	12	13	14	15	16	17	18
21	22	23	24	25	26	27	19	20	21	22	23	24	25
28	29	30					26	27	28	29	30	31	

Southern Fried Chicken

Nothing says Southern cooking like fried chicken, and I think my recipe is one of the best! Capturing spices (and a little heat) under a finger-licking crispy skin really can't be beat.

Makes 4 servings

4   large eggs
$1/3$ cup water
1   cup hot pepper sauce
2   cups self-rising flour
1   teaspoon pepper
One 2$1/2$-pound chicken, cut into
     pieces
House Seasoning (recipe follows)
Oil for frying, preferably peanut oil

In a medium bowl, beat eggs with water. Add enough hot sauce so that the egg mixture is bright orange. In another bowl, combine flour and pepper. Season chicken with House Seasoning. Dip seasoned chicken in egg mixture, then coat well with flour mixture.

    Pour oil into a deep pot, making sure not to fill it more than halfway. Heat to 350°F.

    Fry the chicken in oil until browned and crisp. Dark meat takes longer than white meat. It should take dark meat about 13 to 14 minutes, white meat around 8 to 10 minutes.

House Seasoning
Makes about 1$1/2$ cups

1   cup salt
$1/4$ cup black pepper
$1/4$ cup garlic powder

Combine all ingredients, and store in an airtight container for up to 6 months.

July

Monday 6

National Fried Chicken Day

Tuesday 7

Wednesday 8

Thursday 9

Friday 10

Saturday 11

Beat the heat with some homemade ice cream.

Sunday 12

	July							August					
S	M	T	W	T	F	S	S	M	T	W	T	F	S
			1	2	3	4							1
5	6	7	8	9	10	11	2	3	4	5	6	7	8
12	13	14	15	16	17	18	9	10	11	12	13	14	15
19	20	21	22	23	24	25	16	17	18	19	20	21	22
26	27	28	29	30	31		23	24	25	26	27	28	29
							30	31					

Picnic on the Boat

One of the best things about Savannah is being so close to the water. The Deen-Groover family loves going out on the boat for an afternoon sail with our very own Captain Michael. In fact, one reason I fell in love with Michael was because he taught me how to operate my boat when I couldn't even begin to turn that thing on! I knew I'd enjoy having one since I lived on the water, but I didn't know the first thing about being a captain! Our earliest memories as neighbors (right before we became a couple) are of us riding around on the water, talking and giggling and getting to know each other. Michael did the hard work while I just looked out at the water and his cute face. I know now that I make a much better first mate than a captain!

Cruising on the water is still a special weekend event. We all make something for a picnic lunch on the boat and throw on our bathing suits in the summer or a pair of comfy jeans in the fall. There's no better feeling than a little sunshine on your face, some wind in your sails, and a whole lot of good food and laughs.

July

Monday 13

Tuesday 14

Wednesday 15

Thursday 16

Friday 17

Saturday 18

Pack up the family for a picnic at the park.

Sunday 19

July								August					
S	M	T	W	T	F	S	S	M	T	W	T	F	S
			1	2	3	4							1
5	6	7	8	9	10	11	2	3	4	5	6	7	8
12	13	14	15	16	17	18	9	10	11	12	13	14	15
19	20	21	22	23	24	25	16	17	18	19	20	21	22
26	27	28	29	30	31		23	24	25	26	27	28	29
							30	31					

Broccoli and Cabbage Slaw

*Slaw is an essential side for summertime cookouts,
and this sweet-and-tangy recipe sure fills the bill.*

MAKES 10 SERVINGS

Two 3-ounce packages beef-flavored
    ramen noodles
1   cup slivered almonds
One 16-ounce bag angel hair shredded
    cabbage
One 10-ounce bag broccoli slaw mix
³/₄ cup sliced green onions
1   cup vegetable oil
¹/₂ cup sugar
¹/₃ cup rice wine vinegar

Preheat oven to 400°F. Break ramen noodles into small pieces, and reserve the seasoning packets. On a large baking sheet, combine ramen noodles and almonds. Cook 6 to 8 minutes, stirring occasionally, until lightly browned; set aside.

In a large bowl, combine shredded cabbage, broccoli slaw, and green onions.

In a small bowl, combine oil, sugar, vinegar, and ramen noodle seasoning packets. Pour over slaw mix. Stir in noodles and almonds. Serve immediately.

July

Monday 20

Tuesday 21

Wednesday 22

Thursday 23

Put a few wildflowers in a jar for tonight's dinner table.

Friday 24

Saturday 25

Sunday 26

July							August						
S	M	T	W	T	F	S	S	M	T	W	T	F	S
			1	2	3	4							1
5	6	7	8	9	10	11	2	3	4	5	6	7	8
12	13	14	15	16	17	18	9	10	11	12	13	14	15
19	20	21	22	23	24	25	16	17	18	19	20	21	22
26	27	28	29	30	31		23	24	25	26	27	28	29
							30	31					

4th of July Cupcakes

Sugar-cookie-and-sprinkle-topped cupcakes—kids and grown-ups will be fighting for these festive treats.

MAKES 24 CUPCAKES

One 18.25-ounce box red velvet cake mix
One 3.9-ounce box instant chocolate pudding mix
1   cup sour cream
$\frac{1}{2}$ cup water
$\frac{1}{2}$ cup vegetable oil
3   large eggs
One 12-ounce can cream cheese icing
Garnish: sugar sprinkles and nonpareils
Star Sugar Cookies (recipe follows)

Preheat oven to 350°F.

In a large bowl, combine cake mix and next 5 ingredients. Beat with an electric mixer at low speed 1 minute, or until dry ingredients are moistened. Beat at medium speed 2 minutes.

Line two 12-cup muffin pans with paper liners. Fill cups two-thirds full with batter. Bake 18 to 20 minutes, or until a tester inserted in center comes out clean. Let cool completely on wire racks. Spread cream cheese icing evenly over each cupcake. Sprinkle with nonpareils and sugar sprinkles. Place 2 Star Sugar Cookies, undecorated sides together, in each cupcake.

Star Sugar Cookies
MAKES ABOUT 5 DOZEN

Two 18-ounce packages refrigerated sugar-cookie dough
48   flat wooden toothpicks
Colored sugar sprinkles

Preheat oven to 350°F. Lightly grease cookie sheets.

On a lightly floured surface, roll out dough to $\frac{1}{4}$-inch thickness. Cut with a 2-inch star-shaped cookie cutter.

On a prepared cookie sheet, place 1 toothpick. Set cut-out cookie on top third of toothpick, with the top point of the star pointing away from you. Repeat procedure with remaining toothpicks and cut-out cookies. Sprinkle with colored sugar sprinkles.

Bake 10 to 12 minutes, or until lightly browned. Let cool on cookie sheets 2 minutes. Remove to wire racks to cool completely. Store cookies uncovered (cookies will get soft if covered, and toothpicks won't stay in when you try to stand them in the cupcakes).

Monday 27

_____

Tuesday 28

Take your dogs for a long walk.

_____

Wednesday 29

_____

Thursday 30

_____

Friday 31

_____

Saturday 1

_____

Sunday 2

National Ice Cream Sandwich Day

July							August						
S	M	T	W	T	F	S	S	M	T	W	T	F	S
			1	2	3	4							1
5	6	7	8	9	10	11	2	3	4	5	6	7	8
12	13	14	15	16	17	18	9	10	11	12	13	14	15
19	20	21	22	23	24	25	16	17	18	19	20	21	22
26	27	28	29	30	31		23	24	25	26	27	28	29
							30	31					

August 2009

Sunday	Monday	Tuesday	Wednesday	Thursday
2	3	4	5	6
9	10	11	12	13
16	17	18	19	20
23 / 30	24 / 31	25	26	27

Friday	Saturday
	1
7	8
14	15
21	22
28	29

I still remember the excitement of that first day of school each year. It was a time to see friends after the long summer and to make new friends, too. And of course, for me, it also meant I could get back to doing what I really loved— cheerleadin' for Albany High School. There was nothing quite like being on the football field on a Friday night with those cute football players and the stadium lights shining down on me.

I don't have kids in school any longer, but this time of year I always think about the little ones rushing to meet their new teachers. They have backpacks full of shiny pencils, crayons, and other school supplies, and probably a new outfit and shoes for the first day. It won't be long till I'm back-to-school shopping with my grandson, Jack. I can't wait to take him to school and relive all those wonderful days I had.

Shrimp Po-Boys

If you let your seafood market steam the shrimp for you, putting these
tasty po-boys together is a breeze.

MAKES 6 SANDWICHES

2	pounds large Cajun steamed shrimp
1	cup mayonnaise
2	cloves garlic, minced
2	green onions, sliced
1	tablespoon prepared mustard
1	tablespoon chopped fresh parsley
3/4	teaspoon Creole seasoning

One 18-ounce package sub rolls, split
1/2 cup butter, softened
2 cups shredded iceberg lettuce

Peel and devein shrimp; set aside.

In a small bowl, combine mayonnaise and next 5 ingredients; set aside.

Spread cut side of sub rolls evenly with softened butter. Broil roll halves, butter side up, 5 inches from heat for 4 to 5 minutes, or until golden. Spread prepared sauce evenly over toasted rolls. Place shrimp and lettuce on bottom halves of rolls; cover with tops.

August

Monday 3

Tuesday 4

Wednesday 5

Thursday 6

Take a blanket outside and stargaze with your sweetie.

Friday 7

Saturday 8

Sunday 9

August							September						
S	M	T	W	T	F	S	S	M	T	W	T	F	S
						1			1	2	3	4	5
2	3	4	5	6	7	8	6	7	8	9	10	11	12
9	10	11	12	13	14	15	13	14	15	16	17	18	19
16	17	18	19	20	21	22	20	21	22	23	24	25	26
23	24	25	26	27	28	29	27	28	29	30			
30	31												

Red Potato Salad

This summertime staple stands out in a zesty Dijon-vinegar marinade. And since it's best made ahead and refrigerated, it becomes perfect picnic fare.

MAKES 8 TO 10 SERVINGS

12 cups cubed red potatoes
1 cup chopped green bell pepper (about 1 medium)
$^1/_2$ cup minced red onion
$^1/_2$ cup extra virgin olive oil
$^1/_3$ cup red wine vinegar
2 tablespoons Dijon mustard
2 tablespoons mayonnaise
$1^1/_2$ teaspoons salt
$^1/_2$ teaspoon ground black pepper

Cook potatoes, covered, in boiling water to cover, for 10 minutes, or until tender; drain well and cool.

In a large bowl, combine potatoes, bell pepper, and onion.

In a small bowl, whisk together remaining ingredients. Pour over potato mixture, tossing gently to coat. Cover and refrigerate.

August

Monday 10

Tuesday 11

Wednesday 12

Thursday 13

Friday 14

Host an end-of-summer cookout.

Saturday 15

Sunday 16

		August							September			
S	M	T	W	T	F	S	S	M	T	W	T	F	S
						1			1	2	3	4	5
2	3	4	5	6	7	8	6	7	8	9	10	11	12
9	10	11	12	13	14	15	13	14	15	16	17	18	19
16	17	18	19	20	21	22	20	21	22	23	24	25	26
23	24	25	26	27	28	29	27	28	29	30			
30	31											

Lunch-Box Lunches

Save the trees, and bring back reusable lunch boxes! Available in a variety of designs and colors, lunch boxes can be found at hobby stores and most major retail stores. If you want a more retro look, check out thrift stores and the Internet.

Small Hands

Miniature cocktail breads are the perfect sandwich size for little hands. You can try a triple-decker or use cookie cutters to create a menagerie of sandwiches. Peanut butter and jelly becomes even more tempting when spread on puppy dogs and piglets. Substitute small water bottles or juice boxes for the traditional thermos, as they are easier for kids to hold.

Happy Packaging

Since lunchtime is often show-and-tell time for kids, make sure you send them off with a festive presentation. Package loose snacks such as Goldfish® and pretzels with ribbon and cellophane gift bags. To make fancy fruit kabobs, skewer fruit onto lollipop sticks. Also, pack brightly colored veggies for added nutrients. Line the lunch box with colorful napkins, and don't forget to add a love note from Mom. They'll be excited about opening their lunch each day!

August

Monday 17

Tuesday 18

Wednesday 19

Thursday 20

Friday 21

Saturday 22

Go back-to-school shopping. Remember to buy some new pencils and notebooks for yourself, too.

Sunday 23

		August				
S	M	T	W	T	F	S
						1
2	3	4	5	6	7	8
9	10	11	12	13	14	15
16	17	18	19	20	21	22
23	24	25	26	27	28	29
30	31					

		September				
S	M	T	W	T	F	S
		1	2	3	4	5
6	7	8	9	10	11	12
13	14	15	16	17	18	19
20	21	22	23	24	25	26
27	28	29	30			

Southern Pecan Brownies

Lining the pan with aluminum foil serves two purposes with these decadent brownies. It makes removing the brownies simple and cleaning up a breeze!

Makes 2 dozen brownies

1½ cups butter
5   ounces unsweetened chocolate
2½ cups sugar
6   large eggs
2   cups all-purpose flour
½   teaspoon salt
1   teaspoon vanilla extract
1   cup milk chocolate morsels
1   cup toasted chopped pecans
Garnish: confectioners' sugar

Preheat oven to 350°F. Line a 13 x 9 x 2-inch baking pan with heavy-duty aluminum foil; lightly grease foil.

In a medium microwave-safe bowl, combine butter and unsweetened chocolate. Microwave on high in 30-second intervals, stirring after each, until butter and chocolate are melted and smooth, about 2 minutes total. Set aside to cool.

In a large bowl, beat sugar and eggs at high speed with an electric mixer until fluffy. Gradually beat in flour and salt.

Add melted-butter mixture, stirring well. Stir in vanilla, chocolate morsels, and pecans. Pour into prepared pan. Bake 35 to 38 minutes, or until center is firm. Once cool, lift brownies from pan using foil as handles. Dust with confectioners' sugar, if desired.

Monday 24

Prepare a good before-school breakfast for the kids. It'll make getting back into the school routine easier.

Tuesday 25

Wednesday 26

Thursday 27

Friday 28

Time to plan for Labor Day weekend.

Saturday 29

Sunday 30

August							September						
S	M	T	W	T	F	S	S	M	T	W	T	F	S
						1			1	2	3	4	5
2	3	4	5	6	7	8	6	7	8	9	10	11	12
9	10	11	12	13	14	15	13	14	15	16	17	18	19
16	17	18	19	20	21	22	20	21	22	23	24	25	26
23	24	25	26	27	28	29	27	28	29	30			
30	31												

September 2009

Sunday	Monday	Tuesday	Wednesday	Thursday
		1	2	3
6	Labor Day 7	8	9	10
Grandparents' Day 13	14	15	16	17
20	21	22	23	24
Yom Kippur begins 27	28	29	30	

Friday	Saturday
4	5
11	12
Rosh Hashanah begins 18	19
25	26

Although in Savannah we don't see the leaves change like the rest of the country does and it stays warm most of the year, I often crave the cool breeze that slowly comes my way in the late-fall and winter months. Since it's still hot at home on Labor Day, we always enjoy a big family cookout by the water, with lots of great food to eat and cruises with our own Captain Michael. Lately I've been spending my mornings and afternoons sitting on my porch when I'm home. In the peace and quiet, I reflect on another blessed summer and all the opportunities it brought.

Party Pita Pizzas

These easy-to-make mini pizzas are great for tailgating or a kid's birthday party. If you don't like Canadian bacon and pepperoni, use any toppings you choose.

MAKES ABOUT 4 DOZEN PIZZAS

Two 7-ounce bags mini pitas, split
One 14-ounce jar pizza sauce
16 ounces grated mozzarella cheese
One 6-ounce package Canadian-style bacon, chopped
One 3.5-ounce package sliced pepperoni, chopped

Preheat oven to 400°F. Line 2 baking sheets with parchment paper.

Place pita halves on prepared baking sheets. Spread pizza sauce evenly over pitas. Sprinkle with cheese, and top with Canadian-style bacon and pepperoni. Bake for 10 to 12 minutes, or until cheese is melted.

August/September

Tuesday 1

Wednesday 2

Thursday 3

Friday 4

It's the beginning of Labor Day weekend and the end of summer.

Saturday 5

Sunday 6

	August							September					
S	M	T	W	T	F	S	S	M	T	W	T	F	S
						1			1	2	3	4	5
2	3	4	5	6	7	8	6	7	8	9	10	11	12
9	10	11	12	13	14	15	13	14	15	16	17	18	19
16	17	18	19	20	21	22	20	21	22	23	24	25	26
23	24	25	26	27	28	29	27	28	29	30			
30	31												

We Love Our Dawgs!

For a lot of people in the South, fall means only one thing—college football. Football is more than just a tradition or hobby in the South; it's a way of life. The football bug got to my boys and my brother a long time ago. You cannot imagine three bigger Georgia Bulldawg fans than Jamie, Bobby, and Bubba. Never mind that none of them attended the University of Georgia. They're the kinds of fans who had no problem shelling out big bucks for the lockers of former Bulldawg players. The three of them have those lockers proudly displayed at work and consider it money well spent. I guess even grown-up boys have to have toys, huh?

Monday 7

Labor Day

Tuesday 8

Wednesday 9

Thursday 10

Friday 11

Saturday 12

I'm so glad to be a grandmother!

Sunday 13

Grandparents' Day

September							October						
S	M	T	W	T	F	S	S	M	T	W	T	F	S
		1	2	3	4	5					1	2	3
6	7	8	9	10	11	12	4	5	6	7	8	9	10
13	14	15	16	17	18	19	11	12	13	14	15	16	17
20	21	22	23	24	25	26	18	19	20	21	22	23	24
27	28	29	30				25	26	27	28	29	30	31

Vidalia Onion Pie

The taste of Vidalia onions is Georgia's most famous. This sweet onion is grown in southeast Georgia, just a few miles west of Savannah. This pie has the taste and texture of a quiche.

MAKES ONE 9-INCH PIE

3   tablespoons butter
3   cups thinly sliced Vidalia onion
One 9-inch prebaked deep-dish pie
    shell
$^1/_2$ cup milk
$1^1/_2$ cups sour cream
1   teaspoon salt
2   eggs, beaten
3   tablespoons all-purpose flour
4   slices bacon, crisply cooked and
    crumbled

Preheat oven to 325°F. In a small skillet, melt butter. Sauté onion in butter until lightly browned. Spoon into pie shell. Combine milk, sour cream, salt, eggs, and flour. Mix well and pour over onion mixture. Garnish with bacon. Bake 30 minutes, or until firm in center.

September

Monday 14

Tuesday 15

Wednesday 16

Thursday 17

Friday 18

Rosh Hashanah begins
at sundown

Saturday 19

*Harvest your basil and make pesto for the winter. Pesto can be
topped with a thin layer of olive oil and frozen for a few months.*

Sunday 20

September							October						
S	M	T	W	T	F	S	S	M	T	W	T	F	S
		1	2	3	4	5						1	2	3
6	7	8	9	10	11	12	4	5	6	7	8	9	10
13	14	15	16	17	18	19	11	12	13	14	15	16	17
20	21	22	23	24	25	26	18	19	20	21	22	23	24
27	28	29	30				25	26	27	28	29	30	31

Chicken and Artichoke Casserole

Perfect for company or a potluck supper, this casserole is full of good things; the buttery croutons really make it memorable.

MAKES 6 SERVINGS

¹/₂ cup butter
3   cloves garlic, minced
2   shallots, minced
¹/₂ cup dry white wine
1   cup heavy whipping cream
One 8-ounce package cream cheese, softened
5   ounces grated Parmesan cheese
2   cups chopped cooked chicken
One 14-ounce can quartered artichokes, drained and chopped
One 10-ounce package frozen chopped spinach, thawed and squeezed dry
¹/₂ teaspoon salt
¹/₄ teaspoon ground black pepper
2   cups ¹/₂-inch French-bread cubes
3   tablespoons butter, melted

Preheat oven to 350°F. Lightly grease a 2¹/₂-quart casserole dish or 6 individual baking dishes.

In a large skillet, melt butter over medium-high heat. Add garlic and shallots; cook 2 minutes, stirring occasionally. Stir in wine; cook 3 minutes. Stir in cream; simmer 5 minutes. Add cream cheese and Parmesan cheese, stirring until combined. Stir in chicken, artichokes, spinach, salt, and pepper. Remove from heat. Spoon into prepared baking dish.

In a small bowl, combine French-bread cubes and melted butter, tossing to coat. Sprinkle evenly over casserole. Bake 30 minutes, or until lightly browned.

September

Monday 21

Tuesday 22

First Day of Autumn

Wednesday 23

Thursday 24

Friday 25

Saturday 26

National Pancake Day

Sunday 27

Yom Kippur
begins at sundown

September								October						
S	M	T	W	T	F	S		S	M	T	W	T	F	S
		1	2	3	4	5						1	2	3
6	7	8	9	10	11	12		4	5	6	7	8	9	10
13	14	15	16	17	18	19		11	12	13	14	15	16	17
20	21	22	23	24	25	26		18	19	20	21	22	23	24
27	28	29	30					25	26	27	28	29	30	31

Autumn

With cooler weather and shorter
days, now's the time to heat up the
kitchen and cook with your family
and friends.

October 2009

Sunday	Monday	Tuesday	Wednesday	Thursday
				1
4	5	6	7	8
11	Columbus Day 12	13	14	15
18	19	20	21	22
25	26	27	28	29

Friday	Saturday
2	3
9	10
16	17
23	24
30	Halloween 31

*H*alloween is one of those great holidays that's so enjoyable. Of course, it's really for the kids, and that's what makes it so much fun for adults. When the parade of little ghosts and goblins shows up at my door each year, I know it's time to pull out the candy. I think it's extra special to make goodies for my trick-or-treaters, but sometimes I just don't have the time. Instead, I wrap all the Halloween favorites in fun, festive papers and bags. As I hand out the goodies, I see the smiles on their faces, and it assures me that they'll be back for more treats next year.

Spinach-Stuffed Squash

Stuffed squash make a fantastic side for fall dinners.
Serve with a roasted pork tenderloin or baked chicken.

MAKES 12 SERVINGS

6   large yellow squash, halved
      lengthwise
2   tablespoons olive oil
3/4   teaspoon salt, divided
1/4   teaspoon ground black pepper
2   tablespoons butter
1/2   cup chopped onion
One 10-ounce package frozen chopped
      spinach, thawed and squeezed dry
1   cup chicken flavored stuffing mix
1   cup shredded Cheddar cheese
1/2   cup sour cream

Preheat oven to 400°F.

Brush cut side of squash with olive oil; sprinkle with 1/4 teaspoon salt, and the pepper. Place squash, cut side down, on a rimmed baking sheet. Bake 15 minutes, or until tender. Scoop out pulp, keeping shells intact; reserve pulp.

Reduce heat to 350°F. In a large skillet, melt butter over medium heat. Add onion; cook 5 minutes, or until tender. Stir in spinach and squash pulp; cook 3 to 4 minutes, or until all liquid is absorbed. Remove from heat; stir in stuffing mix, cheese, sour cream, and remaining salt.

Spoon mixture evenly into squash shells. Place on the baking sheet, and bake 15 to 20 minutes, or until heated through. Serve immediately.

September/October

Monday 28

Tuesday 29

Wednesday 30

Thursday 1

Plant pansies when the weather cools.

Friday 2

Saturday 3

Sunday 4

National Taco Day

		September							October				
S	M	T	W	T	F	S	S	M	T	W	T	F	S
		1	2	3	4	5					1	2	3
6	7	8	9	10	11	12	4	5	6	7	8	9	10
13	14	15	16	17	18	19	11	12	13	14	15	16	17
20	21	22	23	24	25	26	18	19	20	21	22	23	24
27	28	29	30				25	26	27	28	29	30	31

Pistachio-Crusted Salmon

Crunchy pistachios and an elegant Lemon Cream Sauce make this salmon dish worth a few extra minutes in the kitchen.

MAKES 2 SERVINGS

¼ cup finely chopped pistachios
1 teaspoon minced garlic
½ teaspoon salt
½ teaspoon ground black pepper
Two 4-ounce fresh salmon fillets
2 tablespoons extra virgin olive oil
Lemon Cream Sauce (recipe
   follows)
Garnish: chopped pistachios

In a shallow dish, combine pistachios, garlic, salt, and pepper. Dredge salmon in pistachio mixture, pressing gently to coat.

In a small skillet, heat oil over medium-high heat. Add salmon and cook 4 minutes, or until browned. Reduce heat to medium; turn salmon, and cook 5 to 6 minutes, or until it flakes easily with a fork. Serve with Lemon Cream Sauce. Garnish with chopped pistachios, if desired.

Lemon Cream Sauce
MAKES ABOUT ¾ CUP

½ tablespoon butter
½ tablespoon all-purpose flour
½ cup chicken broth
¼ cup heavy whipping cream
2 teaspoons lemon zest
⅛ cup fresh lemon juice
½ teaspoon salt
⅛ teaspoon ground white pepper

In a small saucepan, melt butter over medium-high heat. Add flour, whisking to combine; cook for 2 minutes. Reduce heat to medium; stir in broth and cream, and simmer 3 minutes, or until thickened, whisking frequently. Add lemon zest, juice, salt, and pepper, whisking to combine. Cook 2 minutes, whisking constantly. Serve with Pistachio-Crusted Salmon.

October

Monday 5

Tuesday 6

Wednesday 7

Thursday 8

Friday 9

A bubble bath and a warm towel can make for a joyous event.

Saturday 10

Sunday 11

October							November						
S	M	T	W	T	F	S	S	M	T	W	T	F	S
				1	2	3	1	2	3	4	5	6	7
4	5	6	7	8	9	10	8	9	10	11	12	13	14
11	12	13	14	15	16	17	15	16	17	18	19	20	21
18	19	20	21	22	23	24	22	23	24	25	26	27	28
25	26	27	28	29	30	31	29	30					

Halloween

I still get a kick out of dressing up for Halloween, usually as a witch. I did it when I was a little girl, I did it back in the Bag Lady days (see below), and I do these days, too. I don't think of myself as a witch (and hopefully no one else does either!), but I've always liked the idea of wearing a big hat and stirring a big pot of potion. I guess it just appeals to my chef sensibilities!

October

Monday 12

Columbus Day

Tuesday 13

Wednesday 14

Thursday 15

Friday 16

Take a walk and let the fall leaves crunch under your feet.

Saturday 17

Sunday 18

October						
S	M	T	W	T	F	S
				1	2	3
4	5	6	7	8	9	10
11	12	13	14	15	16	17
18	19	20	21	22	23	24
25	26	27	28	29	30	31

November						
S	M	T	W	T	F	S
1	2	3	4	5	6	7
8	9	10	11	12	13	14
15	16	17	18	19	20	21
22	23	24	25	26	27	28
29	30					

Baked Spaghetti

Dora Charles, my head cook, my soul sister, and my friend, really puts her big toe in this dish.
In fact, Fodor's Travel Guide called it "The Best Baked Spaghetti in the South."
Go, Dora! (P.S. Dora doesn't really put her toe in this; that's just a Southern
expression we use when someone has done a dish just right!)

Makes 8 to 10 servings

1½ pounds ground chuck
1 green bell pepper, diced
1 onion, diced
2 cloves garlic, minced
One 28-ounce can crushed tomatoes
One 15-ounce can diced tomatoes
One 15-ounce can tomato sauce
½ cup water
¼ cup chopped fresh parsley
1½ teaspoons Italian seasoning
1½ teaspoons House Seasoning
   (recipe follows)
1½ teaspoons seasoned salt
1½ teaspoons sugar
2 small bay leaves
8 ounces angel hair pasta
8 ounces grated Cheddar cheese
8 ounces grated mozzarella cheese

In a large saucepan, cook ground chuck, bell pepper, onion, and garlic over medium heat, stirring until meat crumbles and is browned and vegetables are tender. Drain well.

In a Dutch oven, combine drained meat mixture, crushed tomatoes and next 9 ingredients. Bring mixture to a boil, stirring occasionally; reduce heat, and simmer, uncovered, for 30 minutes, stirring occasionally. Remove and discard bay leaves.

Cook pasta according to package directions. Drain well and set aside.

Preheat oven to 350°F. Lightly grease a 13 x 9 x 2-inch baking dish.

Spoon one third of the sauce mixture over the bottom of the prepared baking dish. Top with half of the pasta, then one third of the cheese. Repeat layers, ending with sauce and reserving remaining one third of the cheese.

Bake, uncovered, 45 minutes. Top with remaining cheese, and bake 10 to 15 minutes, or until cheese is melted. Remove from oven, and let rest 10 minutes before cutting into squares to serve.

House Seasoning
Makes 1½ cups

1 cup salt
¼ cup ground black pepper
¼ cup garlic powder

Stir the ingredients together. Keep the seasoning in a shaker near the stove for convenience.

October

Monday 19

Tuesday 20

Wednesday 21

Thursday 22

Friday 23

Saturday 24

Get your candy and costumes ready for Halloween.

Sunday 25

October							November						
S	M	T	W	T	F	S	S	M	T	W	T	F	S
				1	2	3	1	2	3	4	5	6	7
4	5	6	7	8	9	10	8	9	10	11	12	13	14
11	12	13	14	15	16	17	15	16	17	18	19	20	21
18	19	20	21	22	23	24	22	23	24	25	26	27	28
25	26	27	28	29	30	31	29	30					

Monster Eyes

Even adults will have a hard time resisting these whimsical treats. These candies can be made ahead and frozen for up to 1 month.

MAKES ABOUT 4 DOZEN CANDIES

1½ cups (3 sticks) butter, softened
2   cups creamy or crunchy peanut
     butter
1   cup crushed frosted cornflakes
     cereal
One 16-ounce box confectioners' sugar
Two 16-ounce packages
     chocolate candy coating, melted
1   cup frosted toasted oat cereal
Red gel icing

In a large bowl, combine butter and peanut butter. Beat with an electric mixer until creamy. Gradually beat in crushed cereal and confectioners' sugar. Cover and chill 4 hours.

Shape peanut butter mixture into 1-inch balls. Using a skewer or toothpicks, dip peanut butter balls into melted candy coating. Place on wax paper, and place 1 frosted cereal O on hole from toothpick to make the center of the "eye." Repeat procedure with remaining peanut butter balls, candy coating, and frosted oat cereal.

When chocolate has hardened evenly, squeeze 1 drop of red gel icing in center of each frosted cereal O and decorate the surface with squiggles of red gel icing. Store Monster Eyes in refrigerator until ready to serve.

October/November

Monday 26

Tuesday 27

Wednesday 28

Thursday 29

Friday 30

Saturday 31

Boo!

Halloween

Sunday 1

Daylight savings time ends

October							November						
S	M	T	W	T	F	S	S	M	T	W	T	F	S
				1	2	3	1	2	3	4	5	6	7
4	5	6	7	8	9	10	8	9	10	11	12	13	14
11	12	13	14	15	16	17	15	16	17	18	19	20	21
18	19	20	21	22	23	24	22	23	24	25	26	27	28
25	26	27	28	29	30	31	29	30					

November 2009

Sunday	Monday	Tuesday	Wednesday	Thursday
1	2	3	4	5
8	9	10	Veterans' Day 11	12
15	16	17	18	19
22	23	24	25	Thanksgiving 26
29	30			

Friday	Saturday
6	7
13	14
20	21
27	28

*T*hough every season has its beauty, I think fall is most glorious. I love to surround myself with the rich colors of fall foliage: cranberry, burnt orange, deep brown, and golden ochre. The palette surprises and delights me each year, and in a strange way, it reassures me. Sometimes changes in life can be scary, but fall is a great example of how change can be beautiful. If life seems tough and uncertain, take comfort in the changing leaves that tell us it's just a season of life, a passing phase. Each fall also includes a time of harvest, which reminds me of the bountiful blessings in my own life. I have so much to be grateful for, including all the lovely people I've had the opportunity to meet in recent years. I hope you know that your support and love mean an awful lot to me. This fall, I'm especially thankful that my harvest includes a bumper crop of new friends.

4-Herb Pull-Apart Bread

This herby homemade bread is a lovely addition to Thanksgiving and Christmas spreads.

MAKES 8 TO 10 SERVINGS

One ¼-ounce package active dry yeast
½ cup sugar, divided
1½ cups warm milk (105°–115°F), divided
½ cup vegetable oil
1 large egg
½ teaspoon dried parsley
½ teaspoon dried sage
½ teaspoon dried crushed rosemary
½ teaspoon dried thyme
½ teaspoon salt
4¾ cups bread flour

In a small bowl, combine yeast, 1 teaspoon sugar, and ½ cup warm milk; let stand 5 minutes.

In a large bowl, combine oil, remaining sugar, 1 cup milk, egg, herbs, and salt; beat at medium speed with an electric mixer until smooth. Beat in yeast mixture. Gradually beat in enough flour to make a soft dough. Turn dough out onto a lightly floured surface; knead until smooth and elastic, about 8 minutes. Place dough in a large greased bowl, turning to coat all around top. Loosely cover and let rise in a warm place (85°F), free from drafts, 1 hour, or until doubled in bulk.

Punch dough down; cover and let rest 10 minutes.

Lightly grease a 10-cup fluted pan. Shape dough into 1-inch balls, and place in prepared pan. Cover and let rise in a warm place, free from drafts, 1 hour, or until doubled in bulk.

Preheat oven to 350°F. Bake 35 to 40 minutes, or until lightly browned, covering loosely with aluminum foil to prevent excess browning if necessary. Let bread cool in pan 10 minutes. Invert pan onto a serving platter. Serve warm.

November

Monday 2

Tuesday 3

Wednesday 4

Thursday 5

Friday 6

It's apple season, so be sure to bake a cobbler or crisp.
Your house will smell heavenly!

Saturday 7

Sunday 8

November								December						
S	M	T	W	T	F	S		S	M	T	W	T	F	S
	1	2	3	4	5	6	7				1	2	3	4	5
8	9	10	11	12	13	14		6	7	8	9	10	11	12
15	16	17	18	19	20	21		13	14	15	16	17	18	19
22	23	24	25	26	27	28		20	21	22	23	24	25	26
29	30							27	28	29	30	31		

Cajun Fried Turkey

In the South, we like to fry our turkeys. And once you go fried, you won't go back. There's nothing like spicy, crispy skin and juicy, tender meat.

MAKES 10 TO 12 SERVINGS

One 13-pound turkey
3   tablespoons Creole seasoning, divided
1   cup butter, melted
3 to 4 gallons peanut oil

Remove giblets and neck from turkey. Remove plastic ring holding legs together and pop-up timer. Rinse turkey with cold water; dry well. Loosen skin from breast without detaching it; carefully rub 1 tablespoon Creole seasoning under skin.

In a small bowl, combine butter and remaining Creole seasoning. Fill a turkey marinade injector with butter mixture; inject turkey with butter mixture, at 1-inch intervals, into breasts, thighs, and wings. Let stand 30 minutes before frying.

Heat peanut oil in a turkey fryer to 375°F over medium-low heat, following manufacturer's instructions. Place turkey in fryer basket. Carefully lower basket into hot oil. The temperature should fall to and remain at 325°F. Cook for approximately 45 minutes ($3\frac{1}{2}$ minutes per pound at 325°F). Slowly remove basket from oil. Drain and let cool slightly before slicing.

Note: Make sure your turkey fryer is on a level surface outdoors. Be extremely careful when lowering turkey into hot oil.

November

Monday 9

Tuesday 10

Wednesday 11

Veterans' Day

Begin planning your Thanksgiving menu.

Thursday 12

Friday 13

Saturday 14

Sunday 15

November							December						
S	M	T	W	T	F	S	S	M	T	W	T	F	S
1	2	3	4	5	6	7			1	2	3	4	5
8	9	10	11	12	13	14	6	7	8	9	10	11	12
15	16	17	18	19	20	21	13	14	15	16	17	18	19
22	23	24	25	26	27	28	20	21	22	23	24	25	26
29	30						27	28	29	30	31		

Helping Hungry Homes

I hope when people think of me they smile and think of tasty Southern food. In January 2008 I started dishing out 1 million servings of meat to the nation's hungry. In partnership with Smithfield Foods and America's Second Harvest, I launched the ten-city tour Helping Hungry Homes™ Across America. Our goal is to get as much food to as many needy families as possible. I feel so grateful that my partners at Smithfield are helping me. When I learned about all the working hungry in this country, I realized that I had to do something. Kicking off the tour in Savannah with my husband, Michael, and my sons, Jamie and Bobby, was just the most wonderful feeling in the world. I also enjoyed working with Mary Jane Crouch, the executive director of America's Second Harvest of Coastal Georgia. Other stops on the tour, which began in Savannah, included Philadelphia, New York, Atlanta, Kansas City, Los Angeles, Chicago, New Orleans, Washington, D.C., and Detroit.

November

Monday 16

Tuesday 17

Wednesday 18

Thursday 19

Friday 20

Make out your grocery list for Thanksgiving.

Saturday 21

Sunday 22

November							December						
S	M	T	W	T	F	S	S	M	T	W	T	F	S
1	2	3	4	5	6	7			1	2	3	4	5
8	9	10	11	12	13	14	6	7	8	9	10	11	12
15	16	17	18	19	20	21	13	14	15	16	17	18	19
22	23	24	25	26	27	28	20	21	22	23	24	25	26
29	30						27	28	29	30	31		

Stuffed Autumn Apples

Apple season is here, and these stuffed delights are so good, you'll want to eat them for breakfast, lunch, and dinner—not just dessert. The combination of dried cherries, cinnamon, red wine, granola, and caramel sauce is like no other.

MAKES 2 SERVINGS

2   large Golden Delicious or Gala apples
1 to 1¹/₂ cups apple cider
1   tablespoon butter
1   tablespoon firmly packed brown sugar
¹/₄   teaspoon vanilla extract
¹/₈   teaspoon ground cinnamon
¹/₄   cup dried cherries
¹/₄   cup merlot
1   teaspoon sugar
¹/₄   cup graham cracker crumbs
¹/₄   cup sliced almonds
Granola Topping (recipe follows)
Caramel Sauce (recipe follows)

Preheat oven to 350°F.

Cut ¹/₈ inch from tops of apples. Using a melon baller, remove core, cutting to but not through the bottom of each apple. Hollow out apple, leaving a ¹/₄-inch-thick shell, reserving apple flesh for filling. Place apples in a 9-inch baking dish, and fill apple shells with cider. Bake 15 to 20 minutes, or until apples are slightly tender. Drain, discarding cider.

In a small saucepan, combine apple flesh, butter, brown sugar, vanilla, and cinnamon. Cook over medium-high heat about 5 minutes, or until apple flesh is tender.

In a small skillet, combine cherries, merlot, and sugar. Cook over medium heat, 3 to 4 minutes, or until wine is absorbed. Add cherry mixture to apple mixture, stirring to combine. Stir in graham cracker crumbs and almonds. Spoon filling inside prepared apples. Sprinkle with Granola Topping, and serve with Caramel Sauce.

Granola Topping
MAKES ABOUT 1 CUP

¹/₄   cup honey and oat granola
¹/₈   cup dried cranberries
¹/₈   cup sliced almonds
¹/₂   teaspoon firmly packed brown sugar
1   teaspoon honey

Preheat oven to 350°F.

In a 9-inch baking pan, combine all ingredients. Bake 10 to 15 minutes, or until lightly browned. Pour onto wax paper; cool completely.

Caramel Sauce
MAKES ABOUT ³/₄ CUP

¹/₂   cup firmly packed brown sugar
1¹/₂   tablespoons water
3   tablespoons butter
¹/₄   teaspoon vanilla extract

In a small saucepan, combine brown sugar and water. Cook, whisking constantly over medium-high heat for 2 minutes. Add butter and vanilla; cook 3 minutes, or until thickened, whisking constantly.

November

Monday 23

Tuesday 24

Wednesday 25

Set the table for Thanksgiving.

Thursday 26

Be sure to tell your family and friends how much you appreciate them.

Thanksgiving

Friday 27

Saturday 28

Sunday 29

November							December						
S	M	T	W	T	F	S	S	M	T	W	T	F	S
1	2	3	4	5	6	7			1	2	3	4	5
8	9	10	11	12	13	14	6	7	8	9	10	11	12
15	16	17	18	19	20	21	13	14	15	16	17	18	19
22	23	24	25	26	27	28	20	21	22	23	24	25	26
29	30						27	28	29	30	31		

December 2009

Sunday	Monday	Tuesday	Wednesday	Thursday
		1	2	3
6	7	8	9	10
13	14	15	16	17
20	21	22	23	Christmas Eve 24
27	28	29	30	New Year's Eve 31

Friday	Saturday
4	5
11	Hanukkah begins 12
18	19
Christmas Day 25	26

The holidays and family go together like turkey and dressing. That's why no matter how busy our lives are, my family always makes time together a priority during the holidays. Sure, when my boys were little like my grandson, Jack, the presents and stockings were expected to light up Christmas mornings. But as we've all grown older (my little boys included!), we've come to realize that it's really the love of our family that makes the season bright. For this New Year's resolution, think about spending quality time with your family, whether it's a holiday or not. You'll look back on those occasions with joy and wonder.

I wish you a wonderful holiday filled with beautiful memories and the light and love of your family.

Cheese-and-Shrimp-Stuffed New Potatoes

Cheesy, creamy, and yummy, these shrimp-stuffed potatoes are great appetizers for Christmastime entertaining.

MAKES ABOUT 3 DOZEN

3 pounds small new potatoes
3 tablespoons butter
$\frac{1}{2}$ pound medium fresh shrimp, peeled, deveined, and chopped
$\frac{1}{2}$ cup shredded Asiago cheese
$\frac{1}{3}$ cup sour cream
2 tablespoons minced fresh chives

Place potatoes in a large saucepan with enough water to cover, and boil until fork tender, about 8 minutes. Drain and let cool. Cut cooled potatoes in half lengthwise. Using a melon baller, scoop out centers of potatoes, leaving a $\frac{1}{8}$-inch thick shell. Place potato pulp into a medium-sized bowl.

In a small saucepan, melt butter over medium heat. Add shrimp and cook until firm and pink, about 3 to 4 minutes. Spoon shrimp into bowl with potato pulp; add cheese, sour cream, and chives, stirring until combined.

Preheat oven to 400°F. Lightly grease baking sheets.

Spoon mixture evenly into potato shells. Place on a prepared baking sheet and bake 20 minutes. Serve immediately.

November/December

Monday 30

Address and mail Christmas cards.

Tuesday 1

Wednesday 2

Thursday 3

Friday 4

Saturday 5

Sunday 6

November							December						
S	M	T	W	T	F	S	S	M	T	W	T	F	S
1	2	3	4	5	6	7			1	2	3	4	5
8	9	10	11	12	13	14	6	7	8	9	10	11	12
15	16	17	18	19	20	21	13	14	15	16	17	18	19
22	23	24	25	26	27	28	20	21	22	23	24	25	26
29	30						27	28	29	30	31		

Savannah Chocolate Cake with Hot Fudge Sauce

Rich with warm and fudgy appeal, this decadent dessert is sure to please guests who have a real sweet tooth.

MAKES ABOUT 20 SERVINGS

2	cups brown sugar
$^1/_2$	cup vegetable shortening
1	cup buttermilk
1	teaspoon vanilla extract
2	ounces unsweetened chocolate, melted
3	large eggs
2	cups sifted all-purpose flour
1	teaspoon baking soda
$^1/_2$	teaspoon salt

Hot Fudge Sauce (recipe follows)

Preheat oven to 350°F. Grease and flour a 13 x 9 x 2-inch pan.

Cream together brown sugar and shortening; add buttermilk and vanilla. Add melted chocolate, then add eggs, one at a time, and beat for 2 minutes. Sift together flour, baking soda, and salt, and add to creamed mixture. Beat an additional 2 minutes. Pour into a prepared pan. Bake for 40 to 45 minutes.

Hot Fudge Sauce

One 4-ounce bar Baker's German's sweet chocolate	
$^1/_2$	ounce unsweetened chocolate
$^1/_2$	cup (1 stick) butter
2	cups confectioners' sugar
$1^2/_3$	cups evaporated milk
$1^1/_4$	teaspoons vanilla extract

Melt chocolate and butter in a saucepan over very low heat. Stir in confectioners' sugar, alternating with evaporated milk, blending well. Bring to a boil over medium heat, stirring constantly. Cook and stir until mixture becomes thick and creamy, about 8 minutes. Stir in vanilla. Serve warm over cake.

December

Monday 7

Tuesday 8

Wednesday 9

Wrap presents once a week so the job doesn't get overwhelming as Christmas approaches.

Thursday 10

Friday 11

Saturday 12

Hanukkah begins
at sundown

Sunday 13

December							January						
S	M	T	W	T	F	S	S	M	T	W	T	F	S
		1	2	3	4	5						1	2
6	7	8	9	10	11	12	3	4	5	6	7	8	9
13	14	15	16	17	18	19	10	11	12	13	14	15	16
20	21	22	23	24	25	26	17	18	19	20	21	22	23
27	28	29	30	31			24	25	26	27	28	29	30
							31						

Christmas Shopping

The hustle and bustle of the crowd and finding that "just right" present are what make Christmas shopping exciting to me. But for some, the experience can be stressful. My advice to those folks is to make a day of it.

Rather than trying to fit it between all your other holiday activities, allow a full day just for shopping. Invite a friend to join you, and start early. Make plans for lunch at a favorite restaurant. When the day is done, you will have finished your shopping and shared a nice meal with a friend.

December

Monday 14

Tuesday 15

Wednesday 16

Thursday 17

Friday 18

Deliver presents to neighbors and friends.

Saturday 19

Sunday 20

December						
S	M	T	W	T	F	S
		1	2	3	4	5
6	7	8	9	10	11	12
13	14	15	16	17	18	19
20	21	22	23	24	25	26
27	28	29	30	31		

January						
S	M	T	W	T	F	S
					1	2
3	4	5	6	7	8	9
10	11	12	13	14	15	16
17	18	19	20	21	22	23
24	25	26	27	28	29	30
31						

Cinnamon Roll Cookies

Nothing says Christmas quite like cinnamon cookies. Make these with your children or grandchildren, and let them share with friends—and Santa.

MAKES 3¹/₂ DOZEN COOKIES

1¹/₄ cups plus 2 tablespoons sugar, divided
³/₄ cup (1¹/₂ sticks) butter, softened
1 large egg
1 teaspoon vanilla extract
1³/₄ cups all-purpose flour
1 teaspoon baking soda
¹/₄ teaspoon salt
2 tablespoons chopped pecans
1 teaspoon ground cinnamon

In a large bowl, beat 1¹/₄ cups sugar and butter at medium speed with an electric mixer until creamy. Beat in egg and vanilla.

In a small bowl, combine flour, baking soda, and salt. Gradually add to sugar mixture, beating well. Cover and refrigerate dough for 1 hour.

On a lightly floured surface, roll dough into an 18 x 10-inch rectangle.

In a small bowl, combine 2 tablespoons sugar, pecans, and cinnamon. Sprinkle evenly over cookie dough, pressing down gently with hands. Roll up your dough, beginning with long side, jelly-roll fashion. Place roll seam side down. Wrap in heavy-duty plastic wrap and refrigerate for 2 hours to overnight.

Preheat oven to 350°F. Lightly grease baking sheets.

Cut dough into ¹/₂-inch slices and place on prepared baking sheets. Bake for 10 to 12 minutes, or until lightly browned. Let cool for 2 minutes on baking sheets. Remove to wire racks to cool completely.

December

Monday 21

First Day of Winter

Tuesday 22

Wednesday 23

Thursday 24

Christmas Eve

Friday 25

Merry Christmas!

Christmas Day

Saturday 26

Sunday 27

December							January						
S	M	T	W	T	F	S	S	M	T	W	T	F	S
		1	2	3	4	5						1	2
6	7	8	9	10	11	12	3	4	5	6	7	8	9
13	14	15	16	17	18	19	10	11	12	13	14	15	16
20	21	22	23	24	25	26	17	18	19	20	21	22	23
27	28	29	30	31			24	25	26	27	28	29	30
							31						

Cranberry Pineapple Punch

Sweet and fruity as can be, punch is the ideal beverage to round off a holiday meal.

MAKES 5 QUARTS

3 cups cranberry juice
One 46-ounce can pineapple juice
One 12-ounce can frozen
    lemonade concentrate, undiluted
One 2-liter bottle ginger ale, chilled
Fresh lemon slices

Combine first 3 ingredients in a large bowl. Cover and chill. Add ginger ale before serving. Garnish with lemon slices.

December/January

Monday 28

Tuesday 29

Wednesday 30

Legend has it that you'll have bad luck if you don't take your
Christmas decorations down before the New Year.

Thursday 31

Toast 2010 at midnight and share a New Year's kiss.

New Year's Eve

Friday 1

New Year's Day

Saturday 2

Sunday 3

December							January						
S	M	T	W	T	F	S	S	M	T	W	T	F	S
		1	2	3	4	5						1	2
6	7	8	9	10	11	12	3	4	5	6	7	8	9
13	14	15	16	17	18	19	10	11	12	13	14	15	16
20	21	22	23	24	25	26	17	18	19	20	21	22	23
27	28	29	30	31			24	25	26	27	28	29	30
							31						

2008

JANUARY
S	M	T	W	T	F	S
		1	2	3	4	5
6	7	8	9	10	11	12
13	14	15	16	17	18	19
20	21	22	23	24	25	26
27	28	29	30	31		

FEBRUARY
S	M	T	W	T	F	S
					1	2
3	4	5	6	7	8	9
10	11	12	13	14	15	16
17	18	19	20	21	22	23
24	25	26	27	28	29	

MARCH
S	M	T	W	T	F	S
						1
2	3	4	5	6	7	8
9	10	11	12	13	14	15
16	17	18	19	20	21	22
23	24	25	26	27	28	29
30	31					

APRIL
S	M	T	W	T	F	S
		1	2	3	4	5
6	7	8	9	10	11	12
13	14	15	16	17	18	19
20	21	22	23	24	25	26
27	28	29	30			

MAY
S	M	T	W	T	F	S
				1	2	3
4	5	6	7	8	9	10
11	12	13	14	15	16	17
18	19	20	21	22	23	24
25	26	27	28	29	30	31

JUNE
S	M	T	W	T	F	S
1	2	3	4	5	6	7
8	9	10	11	12	13	14
15	16	17	18	19	20	21
22	23	24	25	26	27	28
29	30					

JULY
S	M	T	W	T	F	S
		1	2	3	4	5
6	7	8	9	10	11	12
13	14	15	16	17	18	19
20	21	22	23	24	25	26
27	28	29	30	31		

AUGUST
S	M	T	W	T	F	S
					1	2
3	4	5	6	7	8	9
10	11	12	13	14	15	16
17	18	19	20	21	22	23
24	25	26	27	28	29	30
31						

SEPTEMBER
S	M	T	W	T	F	S
	1	2	3	4	5	6
7	8	9	10	11	12	13
14	15	16	17	18	19	20
21	22	23	24	25	26	27
28	29	30				

OCTOBER
S	M	T	W	T	F	S
			1	2	3	4
5	6	7	8	9	10	11
12	13	14	15	16	17	18
19	20	21	22	23	24	25
26	27	28	29	30	31	

NOVEMBER
S	M	T	W	T	F	S
						1
2	3	4	5	6	7	8
9	10	11	12	13	14	15
16	17	18	19	20	21	22
23	24	25	26	27	28	29
30						

DECEMBER
S	M	T	W	T	F	S
	1	2	3	4	5	6
7	8	9	10	11	12	13
14	15	16	17	18	19	20
21	22	23	24	25	26	27
28	29	30	31			

2009

JANUARY
S	M	T	W	T	F	S
				1	2	3
4	5	6	7	8	9	10
11	12	13	14	15	16	17
18	19	20	21	22	23	24
25	26	27	28	29	30	31

FEBRUARY
S	M	T	W	T	F	S
1	2	3	4	5	6	7
8	9	10	11	12	13	14
15	16	17	18	19	20	21
22	23	24	25	26	27	28

MARCH
S	M	T	W	T	F	S
1	2	3	4	5	6	7
8	9	10	11	12	13	14
15	16	17	18	19	20	21
22	23	24	25	26	27	28
29	30	31				

APRIL
S	M	T	W	T	F	S
			1	2	3	4
5	6	7	8	9	10	11
12	13	14	15	16	17	18
19	20	21	22	23	24	25
26	27	28	29	30		

MAY
S	M	T	W	T	F	S
					1	2
3	4	5	6	7	8	9
10	11	12	13	14	15	16
17	18	19	20	21	22	23
24	25	26	27	28	29	30
31						

JUNE
S	M	T	W	T	F	S
	1	2	3	4	5	6
7	8	9	10	11	12	13
14	15	16	17	18	19	20
21	22	23	24	25	26	27
28	29	30				

JULY
S	M	T	W	T	F	S
			1	2	3	4
5	6	7	8	9	10	11
12	13	14	15	16	17	18
19	20	21	22	23	24	25
26	27	28	29	30	31	

AUGUST
S	M	T	W	T	F	S
						1
2	3	4	5	6	7	8
9	10	11	12	13	14	15
16	17	18	19	20	21	22
23	24	25	26	27	28	29
30	31					

SEPTEMBER
S	M	T	W	T	F	S
		1	2	3	4	5
6	7	8	9	10	11	12
13	14	15	16	17	18	19
20	21	22	23	24	25	26
27	28	29	30			

OCTOBER
S	M	T	W	T	F	S
				1	2	3
4	5	6	7	8	9	10
11	12	13	14	15	16	17
18	19	20	21	22	23	24
25	26	27	28	29	30	31

NOVEMBER
S	M	T	W	T	F	S
1	2	3	4	5	6	7
8	9	10	11	12	13	14
15	16	17	18	19	20	21
22	23	24	25	26	27	28
29	30					

DECEMBER
S	M	T	W	T	F	S
		1	2	3	4	5
6	7	8	9	10	11	12
13	14	15	16	17	18	19
20	21	22	23	24	25	26
27	28	29	30	31		

2010

JANUARY
S	M	T	W	T	F	S
					1	2
3	4	5	6	7	8	9
10	11	12	13	14	15	16
17	18	19	20	21	22	23
24	25	26	27	28	29	30
31						

FEBRUARY
S	M	T	W	T	F	S
	1	2	3	4	5	6
7	8	9	10	11	12	13
14	15	16	17	18	19	20
21	22	23	24	25	26	27
28						

MARCH
S	M	T	W	T	F	S
	1	2	3	4	5	6
7	8	9	10	11	12	13
14	15	16	17	18	19	20
21	22	23	24	25	26	27
28	29	30	31			

APRIL
S	M	T	W	T	F	S
				1	2	3
4	5	6	7	8	9	10
11	12	13	14	15	16	17
18	19	20	21	22	23	24
25	26	27	28	29	30	

MAY
S	M	T	W	T	F	S
						1
2	3	4	5	6	7	8
9	10	11	12	13	14	15
16	17	18	19	20	21	22
23	24	25	26	27	28	29
30	31					

JUNE
S	M	T	W	T	F	S
		1	2	3	4	5
6	7	8	9	10	11	12
13	14	15	16	17	18	19
20	21	22	23	24	25	26
27	28	29	30			

JULY
S	M	T	W	T	F	S
				1	2	3
4	5	6	7	8	9	10
11	12	13	14	15	16	17
18	19	20	21	22	23	24
25	26	27	28	29	30	31

AUGUST
S	M	T	W	T	F	S
1	2	3	4	5	6	7
8	9	10	11	12	13	14
15	16	17	18	19	20	21
22	23	24	25	26	27	28
29	30	31				

SEPTEMBER
S	M	T	W	T	F	S
			1	2	3	4
5	6	7	8	9	10	11
12	13	14	15	16	17	18
19	20	21	22	23	24	25
26	27	28	29	30		

OCTOBER
S	M	T	W	T	F	S
					1	2
3	4	5	6	7	8	9
10	11	12	13	14	15	16
17	18	19	20	21	22	23
24	25	26	27	28	29	30
31						

NOVEMBER
S	M	T	W	T	F	S
	1	2	3	4	5	6
7	8	9	10	11	12	13
14	15	16	17	18	19	20
21	22	23	24	25	26	27
28	29	30				

DECEMBER
S	M	T	W	T	F	S
			1	2	3	4
5	6	7	8	9	10	11
12	13	14	15	16	17	18
19	20	21	22	23	24	25
26	27	28	29	30	31	

2011

JANUARY
S	M	T	W	T	F	S
						1
2	3	4	5	6	7	8
9	10	11	12	13	14	15
16	17	18	19	20	21	22
23	24	25	26	27	28	29
30	31					

FEBRUARY
S	M	T	W	T	F	S
		1	2	3	4	5
6	7	8	9	10	11	12
13	14	15	16	17	18	19
20	21	22	23	24	25	26
27	28					

MARCH
S	M	T	W	T	F	S
		1	2	3	4	5
6	7	8	9	10	11	12
13	14	15	16	17	18	19
20	21	22	23	24	25	26
27	28	29	30	31		

APRIL
S	M	T	W	T	F	S
					1	2
3	4	5	6	7	8	9
10	11	12	13	14	15	16
17	18	19	20	21	22	23
24	25	26	27	28	29	30

MAY
S	M	T	W	T	F	S
1	2	3	4	5	6	7
8	9	10	11	12	13	14
15	16	17	18	19	20	21
22	23	24	25	26	27	28
29	30	31				

JUNE
S	M	T	W	T	F	S
			1	2	3	4
5	6	7	8	9	10	11
12	13	14	15	16	17	18
19	20	21	22	23	24	25
26	27	28	29	30		

JULY
S	M	T	W	T	F	S
					1	2
3	4	5	6	7	8	9
10	11	12	13	14	15	16
17	18	19	20	21	22	23
24	25	26	27	28	29	30
31						

AUGUST
S	M	T	W	T	F	S
	1	2	3	4	5	6
7	8	9	10	11	12	13
14	15	16	17	18	19	20
21	22	23	24	25	26	27
28	29	30	31			

SEPTEMBER
S	M	T	W	T	F	S
				1	2	3
4	5	6	7	8	9	10
11	12	13	14	15	16	17
18	19	20	21	22	23	24
25	26	27	28	29	30	

OCTOBER
S	M	T	W	T	F	S
						1
2	3	4	5	6	7	8
9	10	11	12	13	14	15
16	17	18	19	20	21	22
23	24	25	26	27	28	29
30	31					

NOVEMBER
S	M	T	W	T	F	S
		1	2	3	4	5
6	7	8	9	10	11	12
13	14	15	16	17	18	19
20	21	22	23	24	25	26
27	28	29	30			

DECEMBER
S	M	T	W	T	F	S
				1	2	3
4	5	6	7	8	9	10
11	12	13	14	15	16	17
18	19	20	21	22	23	24
25	26	27	28	29	30	31

About the Author

PAULA DEEN is the bestselling author of *Paula Deen Celebrates!; Paula Deen & Friends: Living It Up, Southern Style; Paula Deen's Kitchen Classics;* and other books. She is the host of the Food Network's *Paula's Home Cooking* and *Paula's Party* and has appeared on *Good Morning America, Today, Fox & Friends, The Ellen DeGeneres Show, The Tonight Show with Jay Leno, The Martha Stewart Show,* and *The Oprah Winfrey Show.* She lives with her family in Savannah, Georgia.

Subscribe today and save!

Notes

Notes

Notes

Notes

Notes

Notes

Notes

Notes

Notes

_____

_____

_____

_____

_____

_____

_____

_____

_____

_____

_____

_____

_____

_____

_____

_____

_____

_____

_____

_____

_____

_____

Notes

Notes